Feel, Behave, Think

The Pathway to Human Decision Making

Todd Trautz

D1407286

maru/

2021

ISBN 978-1-7779170-0-5

Book design by Emineh Babayan
Cover design by Wysp Creative
Author photo by John Weight Photography

Maru Group
Toronto, Canada

www.marugroup.net

Table of Contents

Introduction

Before I began writing this book, I had been speaking and writing about the human decision process as part of my work in brand and consumer insights for quite some time. In my previous work as a trial attorney, understanding how people behave and how to influence decision required a deep understanding of the decision process. However, writing a paper or a blog post about human decision making is a very different process than trying to tell a compelling story over the course of a book. On my first dedicated day of writing, I sat there asking myself, what information do I have to share that is unique and could perhaps be conveyed in a way that brings both the science and the application to life more clearly? The idea was to base the book on an analytical framework that was well-grounded in behavioral science and psychology and that explained how people make decisions.

There is a wealth of material about the duality of the human decision process, most famously brought to the mainstream by Nobel Prize-winning author Daniel Kahneman in his book *Thinking, Fast and Slow*. Important work was also contributed by neuroscientist Antonio Damasio in his book *Descartes' Error*, which concluded that human decision making is dependent on emotional input. Our subconscious emotional system and its ability to make decisions not only independently but accurately was also explored in Malcolm Gladwell's *Blink*. The list goes on, but what was missing, in my view, in the story I had been telling clients and peers was an understanding of the entire pathway of the decision process. By understanding the complete pathway, people who work with brands either in marketing or research can gain a comprehensive view of the decision process. If we have a more complete view of how people arrive at a decision, then we can influence and measure it with increased accuracy. We can improve our communications when we understand how the decision will be made.

The pathway of human decision making is that we feel, then behave, and, lastly, think.

I often use a tried-and-true law school analogy that was drilled into my head as part of evidence classes: you can look through the keyhole into a room or you can open the door. If we focus on just one or two components of the pathway, we are always looking through the keyhole. We can never open the door until we consider all three components of the decision and the entirety of the process. This is the challenge I see every day in front of brand managers, marketers, and researchers, who focus on what people think, attitudinally, maybe in combination with how they behave, and are left with an incomplete picture. The resulting gap in understanding leads to misinformed decisions and, too often, wasted investments. Failure to account for the entire decision process creates bias and reliance on single points in the path. This incomplete view is why brands and marketers struggle to communicate effectively to consumers and why researchers miss the mark. We look at human decision through our own specialized "keyhole," never opening the door to the role of emotion.

My objective is to provide you with information demonstrating the role and importance of emotion and its overwhelming impact on behavior, and to show that looking at consumer brand and product decisions through the framework of feel, behave, and think will provide a complete view of the consumer decision. This holistic view will enable you to understand and influence the outcome through more informed insights. By utilizing all three lenses, you can begin to close the gap between what consumers say and what they ultimately do.

I will start by exploring the two modes or systems of thinking and how these systems work. We will then look at these two systems in the context of our primal behavioral system, a core component of our evolutionary and social development. We will analyze how the relationship between these two systems allows us to make decisions with imperfect and incomplete information. It is this ability to make decisions at speed that provides us with an advantage as we navigate the complexities of everyday life. The nucleus of this decision-making process is our emotional construct, constantly providing feedback and influencing every decision we make.

*　　　*　　　*

I am the oldest of four boys, and we grew up in a small tourist town on the coast of Maine. My Dad worked for the Navy all his life in the shipbuilding business. My Mom was a homemaker who worked odd jobs here and there as we got older. My Dad would leave before we all woke up and would arrive home promptly at 5 p.m. every evening in time for dinner. This would leave my Mom to keep us boys in line, which was a never-ending battle. Our upbringing and environment were very blue collar. We had one luxury: we could walk about a half a mile to the best beach in Maine. Every night there was a scramble of boys getting ready for bed. We lived in a tiny Cape Cod-style house with one bathroom the size of a closet. You could reach the sink, toilet and tub with your arms spread. Each of us, covered in the dirt of the day, would go through the nightly routine. Someone would be in the tub, someone would be brushing his teeth, and someone would be trying to skip the tub because he was not that dirty. It was a circus, and luckily, in the seventies, naked hippy kids running around was still acceptable. Brushing our teeth was a big deal because two kids could not fit at the sink and, well, kids do not like to brush their teeth. So, teeth brushing was always a focal point that led to some colorful discussions.

Fast forward to 1996. I am newly married. I had left home when I was 18 and gone off to college, later moving into an apartment when I attended law school. I was always self-sufficient; you had to be independent with three younger brothers. I had bought toothpaste and was brushing my teeth when my wife Laura came in with another brand of toothpaste. I had grown up all my life with Crest toothpaste. I remember complaining as a kid, asking for another brand of toothpaste and being told "we are a Crest family." Standing in the toothpaste aisle and picking out a tube of toothpaste did not involve any rational comparisons. I did not weigh the pros and cons of various brands. I did not pay attention to the claims that 9 out of 10 dentists recommended Crest. Tube size, functionality, color, flavor, efficacy: none of that entered my mind. Instead, the emotion associated with my childhood use of Crest and what David Ogilvy describes as the intangible bundle of attributes and emotions that are a brand caused my behavior. I had an emotional connection to Crest, and I chose it. My behavior had no connection to anything rational; there was no thinking involved. I had been buying Crest toothpaste independently for eight years at that point.

All of you who have ever combined households in a relationship know what happened next. I looked at my wife and questioned her toothpaste; she asked, why Crest? I presented all the rational reasons why Crest was better than whatever brand she had. As you can imagine, this spirited defense of my toothpaste brand came as a surprise. I had launched into a full point-counterpoint discussion on why Crest is superior, drawing on every bit of knowledge I had subconsciously been storing up for over two decades. Luckily for me, I was allowed to stay in the house that night.

What had happened? While the decision path was long-term and not a single point in time, I had developed an emotional connection to Crest. I felt something for the brand; it conjured up all of the emotions of growing up in that closet-sized bathroom. The fun and not-so-fun battles of brushing my teeth with my brothers: all of that was bundled up in the brand decision. My behavior followed my emotional connection. It drove my choice. When my choice was questioned, the post-rationalization came in: the "think" part of the pathway. The features, attributes and claims all came to the conscious mind well after the behavior. Because emotion drives the majority of our behavior, it is only when we are asked why we behave the way we do that we think and draw upon rational reasons to explain our behavior. This thinking only after behavior is the crux of the issue. When people in charge of brands or consumer insights attempt to understand or influence behavior, the focus is always on the end of the process, when what we think is disconnected from how we behave and feel.

A more recent short-term decision that I often speak about is my latest ski boot purchase. It was just before Christmas, and my middle son Drew, who is a great skier and super hard to buy for, had outgrown his ski jacket. He is a typical middle child, so easygoing that you have to almost convince him that he should buy a new jacket. While I was looking online for a jacket for him, I started to look at boots. I am a pretty good skier, and I had a great pair of boots. I had bought them sometime in the mid 1990's. The actual year is a family point of contention, but they were a good twenty years old. They did not look outdated, were of solid design, were a great brand, and fit both my sets of skis. There was no rational reason to buy new boots. I had my boots so tuned in—why would I? After a few scans through the boot section, I bought new boots. I felt that I deserved them; I worked hard, and at that moment I emotionally desired new boots. I did not rationalize in any way, did not rigorously compare features, and did not think through what I would do with my old boots. The new boots were my size and visually spoke to me, and that was it. My behavior was completely driven by emotion. It is what happened next that is integral to the story and to understanding the decision pathway. I had now bought myself a redundant set of boots. Would they make me a better skier? No. Were they materially different in any way to what I already had? No. However, the post-rationalized "think" part of the decision pathway began to fill in all of the attributes and features. If you were a marketer or researcher and you asked me why I bought these boots, I would rattle off the moldable lining, the insulation factor, the race boot stiffness, the ability to customize the incline, the toe box, the micro-adjust buckles, and the list would go on.

Absolutely none of those rational features drove the decision. In fact, when the boots arrived, I had to read the manual and marketing materials to understand how they operated and how they were different from the boots I already had. Of course, when my ski buddies asked about my new boots, I told them all about the price, features, and benefits, and how now I really could ski to my full Olympic potential. It is at this last part of the decision process where brands and consumer researchers are capturing feedback: the end of the decision pathway, when our brain is justifying a decision that has already happened. Our behavior is so heavily driven by emotions that we are operating subconsciously; our conscious, rational self is only there to fill in the gaps in order to provide a rational "why." Our thinking is quite literally an afterthought, a byproduct of the behavioral decision process.

I proudly skied on those new boots, citing all the rational reasons I had allegedly bought them for. I took one of my hardest falls in front of my kids that year. They were amazed that I had fallen, and my son Drew quipped, "it must be the boots."

Chapter One:
System 1 and System 2

Two Systems

One of my favorite poems is Robert Frost's "The Road Not Taken." It speaks to me personally in many ways, and it is a wonderful example of the human decision process. Just as "Two roads diverged in a yellow wood," so there are two paths or systems involved in how our brain operates. As we shall explore, one path is "less traveled by," and that makes all the difference.

In his book *Thinking, Fast and Slow*, psychologist and Nobelist Daniel Kahneman reveals the dual systems of the brain, their pitfalls, and their power. Kahneman presents the two modes of thinking as characters in a constantly unfolding psychodrama. Over several decades, psychologists have written about and explored the two modes of thinking and have developed many labels for them. Kahneman adopts the terms originally proposed by the psychologists Keith Stanovich and Richard West, referring to the two systems in the mind as System 1 and System 2. Throughout the rest of this book, I will employ those same labels as they have become mainstream in brand and marketing discussions.

- System 1 operates automatically and quickly, with little or no effort and no sense of voluntary control.
- System 2 allocates attention to the effortful mental activities that demand it, including complex computations. The operations of System 2 are often associated with the subjective experience of agency, choice, and concentration.

When we think of ourselves, we identify with System 2, the conscious, reasoning self that has beliefs, makes choices, and decides what to think about and what to do. Although System 2 believes itself to be where the action is, the automatic System 1 is the hero of the book. Kahneman describes System 1 as effortlessly originating impressions and feelings that are the main sources of the explicit beliefs and deliberate choices of System 2. The automatic operations of System 1 generate surprisingly complex patterns of ideas, but only the slower System 2 can construct thoughts in an orderly series of steps.

The highly diverse operations of System 2 have one feature in common: they require attention and are disrupted when attention is drawn away. Here are some examples:

- Focus on the voice of a particular person in a crowded and noisy room.
- Look for a woman with white hair.
- Search your memory to identify a surprising sound.
- Maintain a faster walking speed than is natural for you.
- Monitor the appropriateness of your behavior in a social situation.
- Count the occurrences of the letter "a" in a page of text.
- Tell someone your phone number.
- Fill out a tax form.
- Check the validity of a complex logical argument.

In all these situations you must pay attention, and you will perform less well, or not at all, if you are not ready or if your attention is directed inappropriately.

While speaking about System 1 not that long ago, I was asked to provide an example. While Kahneman provides examples of process, I wanted to go a bit further into the resulting behavior. A good example of System 1 thinking in action is walking up and down the stairs. There is no conscious thinking about how high I have to lift my leg or how deep the stair tread is. The standard building code requires the rise and run to be 7 inches by 11 inches. However, we do not consciously think about the rise and run or the process of lifting our leg. It is involuntarily, running in the background of the subconscious. In fact, most people are not even aware that there is a standard measurement for stairs!

We walk up and down stairs all the time. Our behavior is following involuntary instructions from our System 1 thinking. Our brain knows the pattern and does not require the attention or mental acuity that would call on our System 2 thinking. There is no concentration, no calculation, no weighing of the consequences of action or inaction.

I live in southern Connecticut and have been commuting into New York City for many years. When travelers arrive in Grand Central Station on the lower tracks, they need to walk up a few flights of stairs to the main level. The stairs in Grand Central are not 7 by 11; they have a slightly shorter rise. The first time someone walks up them, they may be a bit surprised, and for the first few steps they may look like they are Bambi trying to walk on ice. The brain quickly adjusts to the pattern of the shorter step. No one stops and breaks out a ruler or pulls out a pad of paper to crunch the algebra; people's behavior adjusts automatically. I have now come in and out of Grand Central so many times that my System 1 brain has me going up and down those stairs like any other set of steps. What always amazes me is how quick and efficient the System 1 thought process is in adjusting my behavior from what suits the multiple sets of normal stairs I walk each day to what is required by the Grand Central stairs. The subconscious is filling in the pattern to the extent that it affects the physical behavior of going up and down the stairs.

The next time you go up a set of stairs, try to consciously control your foot or try to walk faster than your normal pace and see how long you can do it before your System 1 controls bring you back to a systematic pace. Your brain will quickly realize that it is wasting effort and energy and will defer to the System 1 pathway. Kahneman lists, in rough order of complexity, other examples of automatic activities that are attributed to System 1:

- Detect that one object is more distant than another.
- Orient to the source of a sudden sound.
- Complete the phrase "bread and . . ."
- Make a "disgust face" when shown a horrible picture.
- Detect hostility in a voice.
- Provide an answer to 2 + 2 = ?
- Read words on large billboards.
- Drive a car on an empty road.
- Understand simple sentences.

Kahneman says, "All these mental events occur automatically and require little or no effort. The capabilities of System 1 include innate skills that we share with other animals. We are born prepared to perceive the world around us, recognize objects, orient attention, avoid losses, and fear spiders. Other mental activities become fast and automatic through prolonged practice. System 1 has learned associations between ideas (the capital of France?); it also has learned skills such as reading and understanding nuances of social situations. Some skills are acquired only by specialized experts. Others are widely shared.

"Several of the mental actions in the list are completely involuntary. You cannot refrain from understanding simple sentences in your own language or from orienting to a loud unexpected sound, nor can you prevent yourself from knowing that 2 + 2 = 4 or from thinking of Paris when the capital of France is mentioned."

Other behaviors, such as my walking up the stairs example, are susceptible to voluntary control but normally run autonomously.

Our Primal Behavioral System

Let's explore a bit the innate skills we share with animals. Our perception of the world around us is the primary mechanism that triggers our most powerful response system: our emotions. Emotions provide individuals a basic feeling of whether a situation is safe or dangerous: the fight or flight response.

Biologically, some of the main chemicals that contribute to the fight or flight response are also critical to other positive emotional states, such as happiness and excitement. When we are in a positive or negative high arousal state, what we experience is the difference between feeling euphoria or feeling fearful. Both experiences are given priority in our memory structure to create a strong memory. A fear reaction starts involuntarily in the brain and spreads through the body so that we can physically and mentally adjust for the best course of action. The fear response starts in a region of the brain called the amygdala. This almond-shaped set of nuclei in the temporal lobe of the brain is dedicated to detecting the emotional salience of stimuli—how much something stands out to us.

This same region of the brain activates whenever we see a human face expressing what we call an emotion: a smile, a smirk, laughter, a scowl, pursed lips, raised eyebrows, red face, and so on. However, the reaction is more pronounced with anger and fear.

As neurobiologist Michael Davis describes it, "A threat stimulus not only triggers a response in the amygdala, which activates areas involved in preparation for motor functions involved in fight or flight. It also triggers release of stress hormones to the sympathetic nervous system. This leads to bodily changes that prepare us to be more efficient in a danger: The brain becomes hyperalert, pupils dilate, the bronchi dilate and breathing accelerates. Heart rate and blood pressure rise. Blood flow and stream of glucose to the skeletal muscles increase. Organs not vital in survival such as the gastrointestinal system slow down."

The part of the brain called the hippocampus is closely connected with the amygdala. The hippocampus and prefrontal cortex help the brain interpret the perceived threat. They are involved in a higher-level processing of context (System 2) that helps a person know whether a perceived threat is real.

For instance, seeing a bear in your backyard will probably invoke a strong fear reaction, but viewing a bear at a zoo will not. This is because the hippocampus and the frontal cortex process contextual information, and inhibitory pathways can dampen the amygdala fear response and its downstream results. Basically, the System 2 "thinking" circuitry of the brain can reassure our System 1 "emotional" areas that we are, in fact, OK.

Like other animals, we very often learn fear through personal experiences. We also can learn to fear things through visuals, language, and instruction without ever experiencing the stimuli that would cause the emotion; this is an evolutionarily uniqueness. We can experience an emotion that impacts our behavior without any rational interaction with what it is that would cause fear. In other words, the emotion and the resulting behavior are disconnected from our rational systems.

My father is deathly afraid of snakes. As a young boy I remember being in the backyard when he was digging up dirt in our garden. I saw him stabbing the ground with a shovel, looking like someone had electrocuted him. He was screaming and chopping the ground. I ran into the house to get my mother. My father was sweating and shaking; he told us there was a snake. As we surveyed the scene of the horror, we saw the chopped-up pieces of a harmless, six-inch long garter snake.

It would be hard to say that the behavior that was triggered by the fear he experienced ever passed through any rational, System 2 thinking. My father had never had a negative experience with a snake; in fact, he grew up in the city of Philadelphia, where I am certain snakes were not a regular part of the local fauna. When I asked him why he did not like snakes, he said he just did not like them; he never could explain anything further. In my child's mind, my father's fear of snakes justified my own fear of them. However, much to his disappointment, I, like most of the boys in the neighborhood, came to enjoy frogs, salamanders, worms, and snakes. It seemed the social pressures of boyhood helped me overcome the very irrational fear of snakes.

Summary

The fast, associative, and involuntary process of System 1 thinking is directly wired into the biological and chemical systems that evoke our emotions. The positive and negative emotions operate in the same region of the brain, with similar biological triggers and systems. Just as the emotion of fear can be formed and experienced without any contact with a stimulus, so can a positive emotion. We can learn when to associate emotions and, as in the case of my experience with snakes, change these emotional associations. Even when provided information from our rational, System 2 brain, our emotional response is so powerful that it generates behavior even when the facts are at odds with the stimulus, as demonstrated by my father's reaction to the snake. Fear may seem like an extreme example, but it is an emotion we have all experienced. We can all think of a behavior that we engage in that is a result of that emotion, and I am certain that if we analyzed the behavior on a purely rational and factual basis, the behavior and the degree of emotional response would be out of balance. In fact, most of us would conjure up a story or some reasons why we behave the way we do.

Bringing it Back

When I was buying Crest toothpaste for years, I was associating the brand with positive emotional experience. The Crest brand, rather than being something learned or associated with fear, was instead being associated with the positive emotions of my childhood. My System 1 process was quickly associating the brand through the single biological response system used for both fear and pleasure, and instead of creating a fear response, it created one of pleasure. The emotional resonance of the stimuli drove the behavior. There was no involvement of the System 2 process, much like in the case of how, for a period of time, my System 2 brain provided me with no rational reason to fear snakes. A stimulus that is associated with a positive emotion triggers a behavior within the control of our fast, associative, and unconscious emotional System 1 pathway. Our System 2 "thinking" circuitry does not need to reassure our System 1 "emotional" areas that we are, in fact, OK. We bypass the check-in with our hippocampus and the frontal cortex. There is no need to process contextual information, or for the inhibitory pathways to fire up to dampen the amygdala response and its downstream results.

This process and resulting behavior can also be as immediate as my father chopping up the snake or me buying those ski boots. Both behavioral responses originated in the same System 1 unconscious, but each delivered a different emotion: fear and pleasure. Neither behavioral response checked in with System 2 "thinking," and both behaviors happened in near time to the stimuli. Feeling was followed by behavior.

We can learn to associate particular stimuli with particular emotions, which can result in long term behavior (my affinity to Crest), or we can be influenced by our emotional system to behave in the moment (my ski boot acquisition). Regardless of when the behavior occurs, the emotional response directing it operates in the realm of System 1; we are not utilizing our System 2 "thinking" before we behave.

Facial Expressions: Fast Track to System 1

Let's go back to another example from Daniel Kahneman of a System 1 response: making a "disgust face" when shown a horrible picture. The amygdala region of the brain, which controls fear and pleasure, is the same area of the brain that activates whenever we see a human face expressing what we call an emotion. Just like in the case of our fear and pleasure response, we can learn to associate an emotion with a facial expression as easily as we can associate an emotion with a sign that is indicating danger.

Our behavioral reaction to visual stimuli, such as a human face, sits squarely within our System 1 controls. Recent work by MIT neuroscientists has indicated that the brain can identify images in as little as 13 milliseconds; according to Douglas Vogel and colleagues, "We respond to and process visual information better than any other type of information. In fact, the human brain processes images 60,000 times faster than written text, and 90 percent of information transmitted to the brain is visual."

In order to perceive positive and negative stimuli, we need a system to quickly assess the situation and render the appropriate response: are we too close to the edge of the cliff or far enough away? We rely on an astounding amount of visual data throughout our daily lives. We cannot stop our System 1 pathway from processing visual data; it is a completely automated and involuntary process, happening in the background of our consciousness.

Dissecting into its parts Kahneman's example of our lack of conscious control of our facial expression when shown a horrible picture would show us that the stimuli, processed quickly in the System 1 pathway, call on the amygdala region of the brain to immediately provide an appropriate behavioral response in sync with the emotion, in this example disgust. Even in the course of an event that can only be measured in milliseconds, facial muscle behavior occurs after receiving emotional information from the amygdala: feeling then behaving, within a blink.

Of course, we are all capable of some degree of poker face: the ability not to fully reveal how we feel. Some people are quite good at it. Even those who are good at controlling their facial expressions have certain ticks or tells which indicate what the underlying emotion may be. The ability to control our behavior requires intervention from System 2. Attention and concentration are required to monitor the appropriateness of our behavior in a social situation. We learn when we need to turn our behavior monitoring on and when we can turn it off. I am sure you have all had the experience of a child saying or doing something inappropriate in an adult setting. If you have been the parent of that child, you can feel the horror as you read this. We go to great lengths as parents to teach our kids to access their System 2 in social situations.

The ability to process and understand a facial expression and associate a corresponding emotion is a quick, intuitive System 1 response. Our processing of other people's facial expressions drives our behavior. We can follow our System 1 path and behave in line with the emotion we perceive or call on our System 2 to rationally decide what our behavior should be. The interpretation of the emotion from the facial expression occurs instantaneously and involuntarily.

We see a child's crying face, and we feel concern or empathy. There is a corresponding sadness that comes to the forefront. How do we behave? Our System 1 path immediately engages us to check on the safety of the child: are they physically OK? Our System 2 path may override this behavior and we may begin looking for the parent, the cause of the crying, and visible signs of injury. The next step in how we behave is dependent on more information. The emotional trigger of facial expression has created two paths to behavior.

Human facial expressions and the corresponding emotions we feel is a field of work that has been explored by Dr. Paul Ekman. His research on facial expression began in 1954 and became the subject of his first publication. Dr. Ekman was influenced by semiotics and ethology, and he focused on the human face and emotion, initiating a series of cross-cultural studies of expressions. These studies led to a conclusion that there are seven universally expressed emotions: anger, fear, sadness, disgust, contempt, surprise, and happiness.

"Emotions," Ekman says, "are a process, a particular kind of automatic appraisal influenced by our evolutionary and personal past, in which we sense that something important to our welfare is occurring, and a set of psychological changes and emotional behaviors begins to deal with the situation."

In other words, emotions prepare us to behave in response to stimuli without having to "think" using our System 2 resources. These emotional responses are an involuntary occurrence. We do not choose to feel the emotional responses; they just happen to us automatically as part of our System 1 processes.

According to Ekman's work, of all the human emotions we experience, the seven listed above transcend linguistic, regional, cultural, and ethnic differences. Each emotion has a distinctive signal, physiology, and timeline.

Emotions occur in response to a stimulus which can be real, imagined, or re-lived:

- a physical event
- a social interaction
- remembering or imagining an event
- talking about, thinking about, or physically re-enacting a past emotional experience

Emotionality, however, varies person to person based on our shared evolution, cultural influences, and unique personal experiences. Our corresponding behaviors are also influenced in this same way. The degree to which we defer to our instinctive System 1 behavior or call on System 2 inputs to provide more information on which behavior is appropriate varies.

I have three boys, and I was the eldest of four boys. My wife was the youngest in her family, with two older brothers. When we had our first son, our experiences with children had been quite different. As the eldest, I had been charged with some degree of responsibility for my siblings. When our first son arrived home, we had an elaborate system of monitors so that we could be listening for any cries. He would cry ever so slightly and my wife would be there in an instant. I, on the other hand, would advocate letting him cry it out for a bit: same emotional trigger, two different behaviors. Based upon my experience, the crying did not warrant a strong emotion of concern and a resulting immediate behavior.

My wife was running on pure System 1 response of feeling then behaving. When my second son arrived, he too would cry, triggering the same emotions, but now my wife's behavior was less immediate. The urgency of response was toned down. Son number three came along and would cry, providing again the same emotional triggers. By this time, however, my wife was aligned with where I had been behaviorally with my first son: let him cry it out a bit. It may seem like a silly example, but the ability to adapt an emotional response and to change how we behave based on that emotional input is an important aspect in understanding when we call on our System 2 to influence our behavior and when we do not. We can save the cognitive input from System 2 and defer to System 1 more easily.

We can shape the behavior that System 1 evokes, as I do when walking up the stairs in Grand Central, subconsciously adapting how high to lift my foot on the short stairs, with no cognitive attention from System 2.

The Symbiotic Relationship of System 1 and System 2

System 1 runs automatically, and System 2 is normally in a comfortable low-effort mode in which only a fraction of its capacity is engaged. System 1 continuously generates impressions, intuitions, intentions, and of course emotions. In fact, neuroscientific research tells us 95 percent of our mental function occurs at this nonconscious System 1 level. Only when System 1 runs into difficulty does it call on System 2 to supply more detailed and specific processing that may solve the problem of the moment. This accounts for the remaining five percent of our mental function.

It is not that our System 2 is lazy; it is just a precious resource that consumes a lot of attention and cognitive power. I often explain this odd couple relationship as resembling two professions. System 1 is head of public affairs, taking in information and shaping our outward persona and how we behave in the world around us. System 1 is constantly taking in information that shapes the communication plan. As head of public affairs, it possesses a vast library of options to get us through the daily campaign trail, scripting our actions based on impressions, intuitions, intentions, and of course emotions. System 2 is a very expensive corporate attorney, probably with an LLM in tax, perhaps one who did a PhD program in astrophysics for fun. System 2 knows the rules and can provide detailed and precise information, but getting that information requires a meeting, and for System 2 to take your meeting it had better be a problem worth their time.

System 1 is out there processing information that generates impressions, intuitions, intentions, and emotions, and unless System 2 wants a meeting, those impressions and intuitions turn into beliefs, and those impulses turn into behaviors. System 2 is only meeting with System 1 five percent of the time to discuss what is going on; the rest of the time, System 2 declines the meeting. What results is that people generally believe their impressions and act on their desires. I choose and buy those ski boots and I continue to purchase Crest toothpaste.

As Daniel Kahneman says, "The division of labor between System 1 and System 2 is highly efficient: it minimizes effort and optimizes performance. The arrangement works well most of the time because System 1 is generally very good at what it does: its models of familiar situations are accurate, its short-term predictions are usually accurate as well, and its initial reactions to challenges are swift and generally appropriate."

For most of our daily lives, we are behaving at the direction of the pattern-seeking System 1. Even when we are faced with an unfamiliar situation or choice, System 1 is going to apply a similarity model: how close or far is this from something similar? If System 1 can find something close, then it will proceed and suggest a response or behavior. If the situation is new, System 1 is going to ask for a meeting with System 2. System 1 knows that getting a meeting with System 2 can be a hassle and time-consuming, so it follows the rule of "don't ask for permission, ask for forgiveness." This can get System 1 in trouble because System 1 has biases, and it is prone to making systematic errors in certain circumstances. Sometimes, like all good public affairs practitioners, System 1 answers easier questions than the one it was asked and moves on if left unchallenged. One further limitation of System 1 is that it cannot be turned off.

The Challenge

What happens when the decision and corresponding behavior directed by System 1 are challenged? This is the crux of this book. System 1 has reached a conclusion and directed a behavior, and now here you are with new ski boots and decades of Crest toothpaste purchases, and someone asks you "Why?" Why did you reach the decision you made, what influenced you, and what inputs were important in making that decision? As stewards of brands and consumer insights, we are the ones putting forth this challenge. Well, much to your marketing dismay, System 1 most of the time never asked System 2 for a meeting. And since System 1 was operating subconsciously, calling on an emotional system of inputs and creating patterns that optimize a positive emotional state and enable a feel-good decision, System 1 is hard pressed to find a logical and rational answer. When challenged, the "don't ask for permission, ask for forgiveness" operation puts System 1 in the hot seat. Time to call a meeting with System 2: "Hey, remember those ski boots I felt we needed, and we bought. Well now some brand marketing person wants to know why we did that." System 2 quickly serves up some answers; it is, after all, a corporate lawyer. System 2 provides the post-rationalized features and benefits: "Tell them it was the adjustable canting system, the color, the cross-terrain stiffness, moldable inserts, micro adjust buckles, insulation rating, the brand, the price…"

As consumers, we cannot explain the process that System 1 went through; it was happening in a fast, associative, unconscious, and emotionally-directed manner. When we think of ourselves, we identify with System 2, the conscious, reasoning self that has beliefs, makes choices, and decides what to think about and what to do. While we identify with System 2, however, in most cases System 2 does not take a meeting with us until there is a challenge to the decisions, choices, and behaviors of System 1. The "thinking" of the rational, logical, and reasoning System 2 is occurring after the fact as a way of justifying why we arrived at the decision we made. We cannot explain the process that we were not consciously involved in. On top of that, when we are challenged to explain why, we have the pressures of social constructs.

No one wants to appear irrational. We provide the rationality served up by System 2 to save face. We want to protect our emotional self and to preserve the belief and appearance that we are a conscious, reasoning being who has beliefs, makes choices, and decides what to think about and what to do.

When we ask people why they reached the decision they made, what influenced them, and what inputs were important in making that decision, the answers we receive are for the most part not even inputs or factors in the process.

A colleague of mine shared the following story as we were discussing how kids' behaviors really exemplify the "feel" and "behave" parts of the process and how kids over time develop the post-rationalized "think" when challenged:

"My mother was just back from doing the groceries. As we put the food away, my oldest brother noticed the peanut butter came in a brand-new shatterproof container. He dropped it to see what would happen. It did not shatter like a glass jar, but it did end up as a splatter of peanut butter all over the kitchen floor, mixed with shards of plastic. My mother, livid, said, 'Why did you do that?' My brother, shocked, embarrassed, and at a loss for words, eventually stammered out some lame excuse about testing whether it was shatterproof. But really, he was as mystified as she was. He just did it.

"Was my brother really thinking through testing what shatterproof meant? Did he set up a trial comparing what happened with a plastic jar versus the old glass jar? Did he have hypotheses about what would happen? Did he have markers for what constitutes shattering? No. He just felt mischievous, let the jar drop, and only then pondered the consequences. He felt, he behaved, and only after the peanut butter was all over the floor did he think."

I am certain we can all recall a similar behavior and challenge scenario where we were searching for a rational explanation. Sometimes we even challenge ourselves—so-called second guessing. We struggle with why we did what we did and mentally prepare a rational response. Have you ever wondered why we call it second guessing and not second rationalization? Do we at some level realize that we did not rationalize the first time?

I am not suggesting that we are all walking around behaving with no rational input from System 2 all the time. However, our consult meetings with System 2 are sparse and can occur at different points in the decision-making process or not at all. For the most part, System 1 is in control of when and if we need input from System 2.

We depend on System 1 to manage a vast stream of primarily visual data. We could not rationally consider the millions of data points that reach our senses each minute. If we did rely on System 2 alone, we would be paralyzed by the paradox of choice and the complexity of our environments.

System 1 processes an immense number of inputs through neural shortcuts, which Kahneman calls heuristics. Instead of examining pieces of data individually, we subconsciously organize any new information into associative patterns we have already formed.

Malcolm Gladwell describes this phenomenon as "thin-slicing": the rapid and non-conscious categorization of our experiences into pre-existing mental models. For example, when someone reaches out to shake our hand, we do not analyze this gesture with fresh eyes each time. We do not wonder at the intentions or the meaning implied by the outstretched hand. We behave implicitly and shake their hand.

Houston, We Have a Problem

For brand managers, marketers, and people in consumer insights, the post-rationalized answers provided after the behavior has happened create a problem. We rely on feedback to direct strategies, product development and communications. The disconnect between behavior and what influences that behavior is compounded by our inability to explain why we did what we did. We often say one thing and then actually behave differently. The resulting Say/Do gap exists not because we intend to mislead; we are often just being asked to explain something that was driven by our System 1 pathway.

Our System 1 pathway is centered on emotional feedback. In this next section we are going to explore how crucial emotions are to our decision making. We will also examine the human inability to reach a decision without emotional feedback. We will delve into how emotions impact our memory and what the consequences are on memory if there is no emotional construct. We will also investigate the workings of the emotional feedback loop that subconsciously motivates us to make decisions.

Chapter Two:
Emotions and Decision

Emotions and Decision Making

Neuroscientist Dr. Antonio Damasio studied people with damage in the part of the brain where emotions are generated. He found that they seemed normal, except that they were not able to feel emotions. But they all had something peculiar in common: they could not make decisions. They could describe what they should be doing in logical terms, yet they found it very difficult to make even simple decisions, such as choosing what to eat. Many decisions have pros and cons on both sides: shall I have the chicken or the turkey? With no emotional construct, these test subjects were unable to arrive at a decision. The groundbreaking discovery was that, at the point of decision, emotions are very important; in fact, even in the case of what we believe are logical decisions, the very point of choice is arguably always based on emotion.

What is also remarkable in the work by Dr. Damasio is the differences noted in a patient of his named Phineas Gage before and after his brain injury and how the manifestation of the inability to feel emotions "impacted personality traits that no longer showed respect for social conventions; ethics in a broad sense of the term were violated; the decisions [Gage] made did not take into account his best interest. The alterations in Gage's personality were not subtle. He could not make good choices, and the choices he made were simply not neutral."

Absent the emotional construct within the System 1 process, the subconscious ability to behave was impaired and the mechanism requesting assistance from System 2 to provide information was also damaged.

Rational information could not flow to the amygdala to confirm or deny the emotion that was no longer there. Absent the emotional influence, behavior or decisions became based on wants and needs with no perception of repercussions. Even choices that would involve the more rational attention of System 2 became impaired. The "reason" or "why" behind the choice was absent. Phineas Gage was making decisions and behaving without the emotional lens that tells us a decision feels right, or a certain behavior is an appropriate response.

Malcom Gladwell provides another example of damage to our emotional construct within System 1. Gladwell discusses the inability to utilize System 1 as a result of autism. People with autism find it difficult, if not impossible, to do all of the things described as natural and automatic System 1 human processes. Gladwell discusses a patient of Dr. Ami Klin, who teaches at Yale University's Child Study Center and is one of the country's leading experts on autism. Dr. Klin's patient "Peter" is highly educated and works and lives independently. He is very articulate, but he has no intuition about things. He can focus on what Dr. Klin says, but only the words; he cannot focus on the way the words are contextualized with facial expressions and nonverbal cues. Everything that goes on inside his mind—that he cannot observe directly—is a problem for him. Without a fully functioning System 1 pathway and absent an emotional construct, Peter is perceiving the world through a very rational, System 2 lens. This reliance on System 2 inhibits his ability to feel emotion, make choices, and interact with others. Like Gage, without the emotional construct he cannot make a decision by weighing the advantages and disadvantages. He can only rationally react to stimuli; there are no consequences, and there is no context and no understanding of why.

One of the things that Dr. Klin wanted to discover in talking to Peter was how someone in his condition makes sense of the world. To that end an experiment was conducted where Peter's eye direction was tracked while he watched the 1966 film *Who's Afraid of Virginia Woolf?* What Dr. Klin discovered is that Peter could not follow or anticipate the film's social construct or emotional tones. He could only follow the storyline by focusing on the objects and facts being mentioned. For example, at one point a character walks into a study and points to the wall, asking, "Who did that painting?" Peter could not connect the pointing gesture to the painting. Instead, he simply heard the words "painting" and "wall," and there were three paintings in the scene, which left Peter frantically going from one to another; meanwhile, the characters' conversation had moved on. The only way Peter could have made sense of that scene would have been if the actor had been verbally explicit: who did that painting to the left of the man and the dog? In anything other than a literal environment, the autistic person is lost.

These examples not only highlight the importance of our emotions in our decision making but also demonstrate that without them we would be trapped in a literal and rational world without the context necessary to direct our behavior. The most basic interactions with other people begin with the ability to process and understand a facial expression and associate a corresponding emotion. We behave after that assessment has occurred; if we did not, we would be operating like Phineas and Peter.

Emotion is part of all decisions we make, even those that require the effortful mental activities of System 2. Every decision has emotional pros and cons on both sides. We just do not realize that our System 1 process has quickly done the assessment for us. The assessment is quick and associative, based on patterns of positive and negative emotional experiences.

I go into a restaurant I am unfamiliar with and peruse the menu. Much to the dismay of most traditional researchers, as I go through each item, I am not recording my level of interest on a Likert scale. What I am engaging in is a trading off, separating the known items that will provide a positive emotional benefit (cheese) from those that will provide a negative emotional benefit (cauliflower). Sometimes there are a few unknowns (wolffish?) about which I have no associative data. I want a positive emotional payoff: enjoyment, fulfillment, and satisfaction. I may need the food to stay alive, but that belongs to the rational, literal world. We could all take a menu right now and separate those things that make the consideration list from those that do not. We do not have to engage in an effortful mental activity of cost-benefit analysis. It is all food, and it all provides nutrients enabling us to stay alive, but we like what we like because it makes us feel good. We may explore sometimes, but at the end of the meal any exploration is going to register an emotional yes or no. When you ask someone at the table why they chose the pork tenderloin, the response is experiential and emotional: I felt like pork, I have not had it in a while, they make a great tenderloin, my wife said it is great, I love tenderloin. There is some associative basis that the satisfaction payoff will come. We tend to choose safely and, in the case of some of us, predictably. We do not think about the reduction process used for the sauce, how the meat was aged, whether the watercress is organic, or why the chef paired tenderloin with watercress to start with. I felt like eating pork tenderloin; my experience in the past has been emotionally positive. Sometimes we have two things on the menu that we want; they are completely different items, but the emotional payoff is similar. At the last minute we choose, and of course someone chooses the other item and then doubt creeps in. We felt, we behaved, and now the post-rationalization of our choice comes. We start to mentally defend why we chose one over the other. We hope we have chosen wisely; if it were not an emotion-based choice there would be no concern, but there is, because there was no analysis done, no cognitive reasoning, just a quick, associative behavior based on emotion. So, at the point of even a simple menu decision, emotions are critical for choosing; indeed, they are implicated in all decisions, whether the decision is completely within the realm of System 1, whether it starts in System 1 and consults with System 2, or whether it occurs under the auspices of System 2. Our emotional construct is the gatekeeper to our behavior.

Emotions and Memory

A few years ago, I was working at an agency on Madison Avenue in New York City. My client at the time was a very prominent financial services company steeped in heritage. We were working with them to develop a global brand strategy. The brand and its clientele were aging. The average customer was a white male in his fifties. The competition was capturing the new millennial wealth and the brand was losing equity. In the work that we did around their three brand pillars, we focused in on the impact of emotion. We could leverage the emotional heritage of the brand and reach out to new customers with emotional tenets under each pillar. In short, we moved from disjointed rational product campaigns to a cohesive brand campaign built on emotion. As part of that work, I created several models that quantified the impact of emotion on brand choice. This work spanned about five years and at times involved several agencies. Time and time again we came to the same quantitative conclusion: that the emotional levers were two to three times more impactful than rational levers. As the evidence mounted, I would hear the decision-makers quoting the "two to three times more impactful" in meetings without my prompting. Of course, the creative agencies loved the freedom of working within an emotional construct because there is so much flexibility on how to deliver. I recall very vividly trying to make my point at one strategic stakeholder meeting by quoting Maya Angelou: "They may forget what you said, or what you did, but they will never forget how you made them feel." The impact of that meeting propelled us forward. Somehow in all the excitement the quote became attributed to me. Each time I heard it misattributed I cringed and wanted to correct the speaker, but the right moment never occurred. Some time later I was at a company townhall event where the global brand strategy was being communicated and the quote came up on the screen, thankfully attributed to Maya Angelou. I could see people talking and turning around to look at me. At that moment, I felt both embarrassed and thankful that it had at last been corrected. My partner at the time and I still laugh and enjoy the victory as well as the discomfort of that day.

We do not recall experiences in a straightforward way. Instead, we remember our feelings more than the actual events. The role of emotion in creating memories is a critical component of our pattern-seeing, fast, and associative System 1 process. As suggested by the Maya Angelou quote, the emotional context is what embeds the moment in our mind, not the rational facts. Even as I recalled the story of that meeting, I was laughing to myself, felt a bit embarrassed, and yet felt accomplishment about the end result.

There are three main pathways to create a memory: emotion, place or location, and story or narrative. The stronger memories cross all three pathways. I was working on a paper related to the topic of this book, exploring long term brand preferences and memories and describing how we do not recall rational facts in general or product attributes, but rather the emotional story or connection to the brand. I began researching the topic of 9/11 memories as an example of how a single galvanizing emotional event can shape strong memories that lack factual or rational grounding. These single-point-in-time memories are called flashbulb memories. A national study of 9/11 memories was conducted by researchers at intervals of one week, one year and three years after the attack. The team surveyed more than 3,000 people in New York City, Washington, D.C., Boston, and four other cities in Connecticut, Missouri, and California. The scientists did a 10-year follow-up survey, making the project the longest prospective study of how memories change over time. The measure of accuracy was consistency with what people reported in the survey the week after the attack. From that first survey to the second survey a year later, the overall consistency of the details of how respondents learned of 9/11 was only 63 percent. At the third survey, three years after the attack, consistency was 57 percent. Overall, the content of flashbulb and event memories stabilized after a year.

What is amazing about this body of work is that the memories did not become less clear; instead, more and more specific detail was recalled, and the details were false. The new details were not intentionally false, but people's minds had filled in gaps with other stories, things they had seen on the news, and experiences that were improbable. The factual details were less and less reliable. While the intensity of the emotion declined, as one would predict, the emotions associated with the event became more diverse. People were recalling events with great passion and emotion, yet the factual components of the story were simply not valid. The emotional impact of the event created a powerful memory, so much so that people were building narratives to fit the memory construct.

We see this play out in customer satisfaction work around vacation travel. Before the trip, there is anxiety and excitement. Any touchpoint prior to the trip that is disruptive or negative is going to provoke a harsh satisfaction evaluation. During the trip, the mental state is more relaxed, and people are a bit more forgiving than at the pre-trip touchpoints. The further into the trip, the more acceptable any missteps in service become. At the end of the trip and during travel home, people are weary, filled with thoughts of the thousands of emails awaiting them, unpacking, and the realization that the vacation is over. At this point the satisfaction bar is at its lowest point. Monday rolls around, everyone asks, "how was your trip?" and we recall the most emotionally tangible examples of our experience. We "forget" the fact that we barely made it through security in time to dash for the gate six terminals away, or that the kid behind us kicked the back of the seat the entire flight to the point that we made the decision never to have kids, or that upon landing the line for customs was days long and that same kid was in front of us lying on the floor so the line could not move up. We remember the tropical breeze, clear water, the emotional relaxation of having no time constraints. The story we recall, even if it is not accurate, fits the emotions felt at the opportune time. Our emotions are leading the narrative.

Emotion has a substantial influence on perception, attention, and memory. Emotion facilitates encoding of memories and helps us retrieve information more efficiently. However, the effects of emotion on memory are not always the same; studies have reported that emotion can enhance or impair long-term memory retention, depending on a range of factors. As demonstrated by the 9/11 study, emotions can overwhelm the factual recall of an event, and a memory can build new "facts" that support the emotional state.

Emotional stimuli consume more subconscious attentional resources than non-emotional stimuli. We cannot control our engagement with emotional material. Once we feel an emotion in a setting, we cannot turn it off and un-feel it. Moreover, the attentional and motivational components of emotion create heightened levels of learning and memory. Hence, emotional experiences are remembered vividly with great resilience over time.

Our memory processing can be divided into three stages: encoding (the processing of information at the moment of perception), consolidation (the storage of information in the brain), and retrieval (the moment of remembering). Emotions have an effect at each of these stages. Our perception and attention prioritize and focus on emotionally relevant information; this results in preferential encoding of the emotional information. As a further consequence, less attention is directed toward peripheral information such as the factual details, so that during encoding the emotional core aspects of an event are well memorized, whereas the details of the surrounding context may be neglected.

Emotion can augment the subjective sense of recollection (independent of the correctness of the memory), which can increase the confidence we have in our memories. The vividness of the memory of emotionally relevant events is often taken as an indication that the memory is accurate.

Without a Memory

In the 1950s, a young man with permanent amnesia changed what we know about learning and memory. Henry Molaison, better known as patient H.M., lost the ability to form new conscious memories after undergoing brain surgery to treat his epilepsy; William Beecher Scoville, a Hartford, Connecticut neurosurgeon, removed the hippocampus that lay within each temporal lobe. Henry experienced every aspect of daily life, like eating or taking a walk, as though it were the first time. When he met someone new, he would forget the encounter within a few minutes. By studying him, scientists learned that complex functions such as learning and memory are tied to distinct biological processes and regions of the brain. They learned that the brain's medial temporal lobe, which includes the hippocampus and para-hippocampal region, converts short-lived perceptions into long-term memories. The discovery paved the way for further exploration of the brain network's encoding of conscious and unconscious memories as well as emotions. Like memory, emotions arise from activity in distinct regions of the brain, primarily the amygdala, which integrates emotions and motivations to act or behave.

Henry's System 1 pathway was fully operational, and unlike Phineas Gage in the Dr. Damasio narrative or Dr. Ami Klin's autism patient Peter, who were trapped in a rational world, he had the ability to feel emotion. He had lost the ability to translate the world around him into permanent memories, regardless of the stimuli or emotion. Emotional events are processed in the sensory systems and then transmitted to the medial-temporal lobe and the amygdala for the formation of an emotional memory. When the memory is cued and retrieved from the amygdala, an emotional response is triggered. Emotional experiences leave strong traces in the brain. Memories about emotional situations are stored in both the conscious and unconscious memory, which is part of the reason emotional memories are so enduring.

While the amygdala is involved in implicit emotional memory, the hippocampus is involved in explicit memory about emotional situations. Thus, when emotionally aroused, we form semantic and episodic memories about the situation. We can create a cognitive representation of the emotional situation or create a memory about the emotions. We are recording the emotion in two ways, unconsciously feeling the emotion and consciously recognizing that we are indeed feeling the emotion, which is why emotional arousal leads to stronger memories.

A large body of work has investigated the psychological and neurobiological mechanisms underlying the influence of emotion on memory. Yet very little is known about the opposite relationship: namely, how memory impacts emotion. The death of a close friend or family member, 9/11, the end of a romantic relationship—these are all events capable of eliciting an intense and prolonged state of emotion. In these examples, the emotional experience and the memory of the event are often inseparable, fused together within our stream of consciousness as we ruminate and repeatedly replay the event. The tight symbiosis between emotion and memory is well known.

However, what would happen to the feeling of an emotion if we could no longer remember the emotion-inducing event? Would the feeling fade away in parallel with the memory? Is it possible that the emotional feeling could persist without the memory?

Studies of patients with severe anterograde amnesia following circumscribed bilateral hippocampal brain damage showed enduring memories of emotion despite the absence of conscious memories. The experience of an emotion persists even though the memory of what induced the emotion has been forgotten.

We can feel even if we cannot formulate why we are feeling that emotion. The emotion transcends the conscious mind. We have all been in a situation where we cannot explain what we feel but we know we are feeling it; being unable to express the feeling does not make the feeling not exist.

Circle Back

At that moment in 1996 when my wife arrived with another brand of toothpaste, surfacing my emotional connection to Crest, my emotional memory of my childhood arose front and center. The underlying emotions associated with family—the closeness, and even the struggles, both physical and emotional—became part of the brand. My long-term memory was not influenced by the rational attributes of the product.

I cannot recall the packaging, the tube size, or if whitening was even a thing in the seventies. I could not describe the flavor, the color, or the texture, or say whether the cap was loose or attached. Did we squeeze it or did we roll it? (the latter being the only proper way, of course!). All I can recall is family chaos, laughter, and us boys pushing the limits of my parents' wits. Part of our nightly tradition was brushing our teeth with Crest toothpaste.

The memory involved a series of emotions, and those emotions evolved over time. I am certain I did not feel the same joy, respect, and overall positive emotions at the time I was trying to fight for space and some order during the nightly routine. The chaos was not all laughs; there certainly were tears. I can clearly connect the brand Crest to a specific location. It lives in this image in my mind of a closet-sized bathroom in my family home in Maine. The tube was always on my mother's side of the medicine cabinet, to the left. If we were out of toothpaste in the bathroom, a new one would always be in the linen closet just outside the bathroom door. In my mind, the brand will always be in this location. I feel absolutely certain that if I went home to my parents, it would be exactly in those spots.

Lastly, there is this story or narrative that I have been telling. Strong memories have all three elements: emotion, place or location, and story or narrative. The Crest brand became part of the narrative and thereby linked to the emotions. I did not attribute the emotions directly to the brand. Crest toothpaste did not make me feel that way, but it did become a lightning rod for those emotions, something that I could point to and say this brand was part of the emotional story. How close I feel to the brand is driven by these emotional associations, even though the brand had no active role in creating the emotions. I have no rational connections to the brand at all. I honestly cannot think of any time in my life that I read a toothpaste package or an ad. However, my behavior over the course of decades was and is still influenced by this emotional memory. When I was shopping for toothpaste, my System 1 pathway would subconsciously call upon the emotional constructs both past and present and I would buy Crest without even a look at the other brands and options on the shelf. The shortcut to behavior that my System 1 brain had constructed had positive emotional resonance; it was automatic, subconscious behavior that originated from emotion. That emotion can be preserved as a memory, felt, and recollected instantaneously, or that emotion can occur in the moment.

In-the-moment emotions can trigger short term behavior, like my ski boot purchase.

Just as emotions are important to memory formation, our memories retain the emotional aspects and tend to lose the surrounding details and facts. Why? Because our System 1 pathway does not need the details or facts; it can behave based on how we feel. A fast and involuntary system that works to create patterns can use the emotional construct as a check on behavior, and most of the time that is exactly what happens. We tend to behave in a way that is emotionally positive or has proven itself in the past to be emotionally positive through our emotional memories. As previously discussed with respect to Dr. Damasio's work, when people are unable to feel emotions, they either cannot make decisions or make poor decisions. In contrast, people who can feel emotions but have no memory can make decisions even without the historical memory of what the outcome may be.

Emotions and Motivation

Most of the goals pursued in daily life are emotionally or motivationally meaningful—i.e., we seek to obtain outcomes that are pleasurable or important for survival and avoid outcomes that are not. We do not wake up with a list of goals to get through the day, but our subconscious does. Our daily routine is full of decision points and behaviors that, thankfully, our System 1 manages efficiently without us being aware. The goals I am speaking of are not those lofty ambitions to climb Kilimanjaro or to buy that new Porsche; they are more mundane. I want to have a pleasant day, I need to eat, and I would like some free time in the afternoon and maybe watch a little Netflix. For each one of these goals there are motivations and emotions that drive those motivations, which occur as the goal is being accomplished or not. Emotions change depending on how close we are to the goal. A simple example: my goal is taking the 6:07 train out of Grand Central so that I am home by 8:30. As I hurry down Park Avenue, I may feel anxiety or defeat as I encounter crosstown traffic. Once I'm in Grand Central, I realize that the train is late. I feel happy that I have not missed it, but disappointed that I will now be home later than expected. Somehow the train makes up the lost time and I am elated that I have accomplished my goal of being home on time. Ok, the last part is fictional—a Metro North train will never make up lost time—but you get the point: emotions drive motivations, and vice versa. Simple mundane goals that we may not even be aware of are being impacted by our emotions.

It has long been understood that emotional significance or impact is central to determining the goals around which human behavior is organized. Emotions are an "affective experience"; we feel the emotions, and they can be characterized by physiological changes. Emotions are defined by how individuals perceive, comprehend, and interpret the world around them, particularly the behavior or actions of others towards them. Emotions carry a functional value in physiologically preparing the body for action, permitting flexibility of behavioral responses to stimuli, facilitating communication and social bonding, and influencing cognitive processes including evaluation, memory encoding, and memory recall.

Motivations are similar to emotions in that they also serve to define the relation between the individual and the environment. A useful distinction between the two constructs as they relate to goals is that while motivation is the driver toward goal fulfillment, emotions emerge from one's sensed rate of progress toward goals; the difference between one's present status and one's goal is experienced as emotions. The emotions felt may lead to goal reprioritization in order to maximize goal fulfillment and the expected emotional outcome.

There is a symbiotic relationship between what we want to do (our goal), how we feel as we move toward or away from the goal, and what we expect the emotion to be when we reach the goal. Emotions can turn on or off our motivation to work toward and complete a goal. Emotions are not specific to a goal; they are fluid, and are influential before, during and after the goal process. In other words, what drives or motivates behavior is inextricably intertwined with and influenced by our emotional perceptions.

Motivations are more specific, relatively deliberate, and associated with a specific goal. In contrast, emotions are produced by multiple contingencies, are more impulsive, and are not tightly linked to a particular goal.

Overall, emotions will typically take precedence over motivations. In fact, some motivations are emotion-specific, produced by multiple contingencies, impulsive, and not tightly linked to a particular goal, while non-emotional motivations are deliberate and associated with a specific goal. Emotion-specific motivations will always supersede non-emotional motivations. Emotion-specific motivations can be understood as a manifestation of goal reprioritization resulting from emotion as an indicator of motivational status.

Most of our daily life goals are fueled by emotion-specific motivations. We frequently shift a goal because of emotional feedback, and that emotional feedback impacts our level of motivation. In my example of trying to leave on the 6:07 train, the goal setting does not need to be deliberate or conscious. We typically refer to our daily schedule as a routine, but if we break it down, it really is a series of small, easily achieved goals with predictable emotional feedback that motivates us through the day. What happens when the achievement of our small series of daily goals gets disrupted? Emotions guide us through our choices and impact how we behave. The effect of positive emotion on cognition influences our cognitive flexibility by enhancing and updating of goal information in working memory. We can have a good day or a bad day depending on how emotionally flexible we are and on how much impact our emotions have on our motivation in relationship to a goal.

What we want to accomplish, even if we are not consciously aware that the goal exists, is subject to a cumulative feedback loop that can start with emotion to frame the goal, which creates a motivation, which is influenced by emotional feedback, which can change the level of motivation and even change the goal. What drives us to choose and behave—the reason, if you will—is encapsulated in emotional response.

Without emotional feedback, we are left to make rational decisions that may not be emotionally positive for ourselves or for others.

Inability to Make Good Choices

Dr. Damasio discusses what he calls a pure version of the condition suffered by Phineas Gage in his treatment of a patient named Elliot. Elliot suffered damage to the frontal lobes of his brain as a result of the surgical extraction of a brain tumor. He went through a series of tests over many years; his perceptual ability, past memory, short term memory, new learning ability, language skills, and ability to do arithmetic and to focus attention were all intact. After all the tests, Elliot emerged a man with a normal intellect who was unable to reason and reach a decision.

Damasio provides the following example:

"Imagine a task involving reading and classifying documents of a given client. Elliot would read and fully understand the significance of the material and he certainly knew how to sort out the documents according to the similarity or disparity of their content. The problem was that he was likely, all of a sudden, to turn from the sorting task he had initiated to reading one of those papers, carefully and intelligently, and to spend the entire day doing so. Or he might spend the whole afternoon deliberating on which principle of categorization should be applied: Should it be date, size of document, pertinence to the case, or other?"

What Dr. Damasio uncovers is that Elliot has lost the ability to feel emotions. This loss of the emotion structure is behind his decision-making failures. With the inability to feel, each choice becomes consequence-free. The goal in the task described above is a simple series of decisions; left with only a rational, System 2 construct, Elliot was unable to formulate a motivation to complete the task, and without any positive or negative emotional feedback to his behavior he was left unable to make a decision. This emotionless decision making impacted Elliot's ability to interact with others, as he lost the ability to emotionally react to stimuli, people, and social cues. His ability to choose the most advantageous course of action was lost; despite otherwise intact mental capacities, his compromised emotional construct left him behaviorally impaired. In the course of examining twelve patients with similar prefrontal brain damage, Dr. Damasio found that the ability to reason and reach a decision declined or was absent without the experience of emotion.

Emotionless choices, behaviors without emotional consequences: ponder that for a moment. No emotional feedback system to guide you: only logic and rational thought. As a nerd, I immediately think of Doctor Spock from *Star Trek*. Spock had mixed human-Vulcan heritage, which served as an important plot element. Vulcans do not feel emotions and operate based only on logic and rational thought.

Spock's catchphrase in response to Captain Kirk's actions was always "That's not logical." Throughout the series, Spock experiences emotions to highlight story points and why illogical decisions are made by humans. In the newer *Star Trek* series, Spock is replaced by an AI robot named Data, who carries on the contrasting of emotionless decisions with what it means to be human, i.e., to feel. I digress, but hopefully the point is not lost. Without emotion we impair motivation, which is the precursor to decision making and how we behave. The inability to feel an emotional consequence also leaves us behaviorally impaired. Every decision we make, no matter how small, has an emotional consequence.

Unconscious Pursuit of Goals

We often act in order to realize desired outcomes, or goals. Although people can skillfully pursue goals without consciously attending to their behavior once these goals are set, conscious will is considered to be the starting point of goal pursuit. We like to believe that conscious decision making is the first and foremost cause of our behavior. That is, we are likely to say, if asked, that the decision to act produced the actions themselves. However, most of our actions are initiated even though we are unconscious of the goals to be attained or their motivating effect on our behavior.

In a remarkable experiment conducted 35 years ago, research participants were instructed to freely choose when to move their index fingers while the timing of the action itself, of its preparation in the brain, and of when the person became aware of the decision to act were measured. The conclusion was that by the moment people consciously set a goal to engage in a behavior, the action has already occurred. The act of thinking about the goal triggers the behavior before we can consciously inform our bodies to behave. Our subconscious attains the goal without direction of how to achieve it from our conscious mind. Our System 1 pathway makes the connection between the goal and the required behavior and executes the command without waiting for any further conscious instruction.

Goals can arise and operate unconsciously. Social situations and stimuli can activate or influence goals in people's minds outside of their awareness, thereby motivating them. The flexibility to produce the same desired outcomes under varying circumstances comes from our capacity to mentally represent what we want to do; these mental representations are goals. Our brain is constantly setting unconscious goals for our survival; it is a primary function of our fast, associative, pattern-seeking System 1 pathway.

Goal pursuit is influenced and controlled unconsciously by social features that have become associated with goals, either through direct practice or through social norms, communication with others, or the media. We are really good at observing the behaviors of others, and we anticipate, react to, and even emulate those behaviors even if they are not positive to us. We often do not become conscious of our motivations until after a behavior is performed, and then usually only when explicitly asked to reflect on it.

We also become motivated to initiate behaviors available in our repertoire when goals are represented as desired outcomes. This is the basis of most advertising. We see people laughing and socializing while drinking beverage A and we at some point buy beverage A because we want the portrayed desired outcome.

Say you want a cup of coffee, and I pour it for you. You do not decide on a conscious level to contract and relax the specific muscles in your arm that will enable you to pick up the cup of coffee. You just think about grabbing the cup and it happens. We are able to initiate actions by focusing on the outcomes. The behavior and outcome become associated on a sensory and motor level that resides in our subconscious. Think back to my story about stair climbing in Grand Central. The outcome or goal, which formulates subconsciously, is to go up the stairs. My feet and body execute this goal flawlessly without any calculations, attention, or rational thought.

The more frequently we select an outcome or goal, the easier it is to execute and the more subconscious and automatic it becomes. We will always defer to behaviors within our repertoire when a desired outcome or goal is presented to us and unconsciously adjust the behavior based on our perceptions of the current situation. A perfect example arose while writing this. I have an obese yellow lab that is very goal-oriented with regard to food. He biologically knows when it is close to 5 p.m. He wanders into my office and begins nudging my right arm so that I cannot type or use a mouse. The outcome sought is simple—feed me!—

and his behavior is as predictable as that of a Swiss watch. I am pretty sure that not a lot of conscious thought is running through his blocky head. He is focused only on the outcome and behaving predictably until I give in and feed him.

Wrap Up

At the time of my ski boot purchase, although my initial goal was to buy a jacket for my son, at some point my goal changed and the emotions around rewarding myself and deserving new ski boots intervened, creating motivation. During the ever-so-brief ski boot search, the emotional feedback increased the closer I moved to putting a pair of ski boots in the cart. Emotions drove motivation, and closing in on the goal drove emotions, which in turn increased motivation, which fueled the behavior. After I clicked "buy," the satisfaction emotions of having attained the goal rose to the surface. I had successfully completed a goal that I had not rationally intended to set or complete. My short-term behavior was overwhelmed by emotional feedback; there is no doubt that I felt, then behaved.

So, what initiated the goal change from buying a jacket for my son to buying boots? (I did buy my son a jacket at the same time, by the way, in case you are thinking what sort of selfish man leaves his son jacketless for ski season, especially the middle son.) Was the subconscious goal lying in wait for just the right stimuli to show up and trigger the emotion?

Goal-directed behavior can be primed and biased by implicit and/or subliminal motivational cues, which creates a relatively direct route for motivation. This is what we hope for in good advertising. The seed of the goal is combined with the emotional result. When the consumer is emotionally stimulated to seek the corresponding goal, the motivation/emotion feedback loop is created. The emotional desire for the boots was there, lying in wait. When I saw new boots on the landing page while directing my search for jackets, the emotional trap was sprung. The advertisement of the boots created the initial emotional response, which set loose the goal-directed behavior that followed. I did not consciously know that I wanted or needed new boots, but my subconscious was already moving toward the reward of achieving the goal. Short-term behavior was directed by an emotional construct that occurred at a System 1, subconscious level through the pursuit of an implicit goal.

How does this goal-motivation-emotional feedback loop operate within the consumer's mind while they are considering or buying a product or brand? In this next section we will examine how the emotional feedback loop impacts behavior and how powerful this System 1 process is even in the face of clear and better rational choices. Positive emotional feedback will consistently drive behavior even when the behavior is a disadvantage. We will also gain further insight into how consumers compensate for those choices by tailoring the narrative to rationalize away why they behaved the way they did.

Chapter Three:
Emotions and Behavior

Deal or No Deal

When we think about short-term consumer behavior, we often characterize it as impulse-driven purchases. There is a whole field of consumer insights dedicated to the study and implementation of choice scenarios where the consumer will engage in quick tradeoffs with low risk.

Most of us first experience the impulse aisle as a child in a checkout line at a supermarket: all of that wonderful candy, so close to the cashier, and plenty of time to convince Mom that you need it. As a child, you cannot appreciate the tactic of placing low-cost items in what amounts to a sensory corral for kids. The items are all low on the shelf, typically around $1.00, and placed at the checkout because research has shown that after Mom has dragged three boys through a grocery store, denying every nonsensical purchase that has been served up, she has little fight left. It's a brutal game of "no" and "why not?" While poor Mom is unloading the cart, trying to keep one child in the seat, the other from under the cart, and the third from losing a hand under the conveyor belt, one of the children, usually the oldest, asks for candy. The compensatory laws of multiple children come into play: if one child should receive candy compensation, the others must also be equally compensated. At this point, Mom is faced with an economic decision in an ultimatum game. Pay the $3.00 fee or potentially drag three screaming boys through the parking lot and listen to heart-crushing sobs all the way home. If there were a professional league for this blood sport, my boys would have been champions. I, on the other hand, did a lot of crying on the way home as a child.

There is a field called neural economics that seeks to ground economic decision making in the cognitive and emotional processes involved. The study focuses on ultimatum gaming. An example of this type of game is one in which two players split a sum of money; one player proposes a division, and the other can accept or reject the offer. The players' brain activity is measured with each proposal and decision.

One player in the game is deemed the proposer and the other the responder. The proposer makes an offer as to how the money should be split between the two. The responder can either accept or reject the offer. If it is accepted, the money is split as proposed, but if the responder rejects the offer, then neither player receives anything. The standard economic solution (or rational path) of the ultimatum game is for the proposer to offer the smallest sum of money possible to the responder and for the responder to accept this offer, on the reasonable grounds that any amount is preferable to nothing. However, the behavioral research shows emotions always override the rational solution. Negative emotions arise based on a perception of unfairness, and people will sacrifice considerable financial gain to punish a partner. The acceptance or rejection of an offer triggers an emotional reaction in both players that impacts their behavior, overriding the basic rational path of both players.

A responder's decision to accept is tied to what they believe is fair, and the further away from fairness they believe the offer to be, the more intense the emotional reaction. What is interesting here is that at some point, even when the offer is perceived as fair by the responder, the responder will punish the proposer by rejecting the offer so that neither of them gain. They will do this to convey that they are not happy with the way they are being treated, even though both players are losing money as a result. Emotion is influencing decision-making behavior, replacing the rational solution with one based on an anticipated emotional reward. In other words, our feelings drive behaviors even when the logical answer is apparent. The mom at the checkout of the grocery store with her three boys demanding a candy payoff is in the same ultimatum game: accept the offer (buy $3.00 in candy to placate the children) or reject the offer and have both parties lose, not financially but emotionally.

What we perceive as fair or reasonable is entirely subjective. For the children who have suffered through the shopping experience, a candy treat is very reasonable, and Mom may agree, even if the cost is $3. Mom may also have a different perception of what constitutes fairness and reject the offer, triggering some negative emotions that will manifest into negative behavior on the part of the children. Both parties are working toward emotional parity, not seeking a rational solution. How we feel is more important than the rational outcome, and we behave in a way that moves us toward an emotional goal.

As observed in the ultimatum game research, while the experience of inequality invokes negative emotions, the opportunity to resolve the inequality is rewarding, invoking positive emotions. The rejection of an unfair offer actually stimulates positive emotions. At a neural level, we are averse to negative emotions and activate behavior to pursue positive emotions, sometimes at the cost of an outcome that is advantageous.

But It Was On Sale

Now expand this idea of deal or no deal to the world of the consumer. We all have a subjective threshold of what we perceive as fair and unfair when it comes to prices of products. Everyone will tell you that they like a good deal; not many people will say they like an unfair deal. It is one of the first things we raise when our behavior is questioned, or when someone notices a new purchase. It was on sale and I got such good deal! Did you, though? Our emotions are evaluating the fairness of the offer and in turn driving the behavior. We emotionally process the offer, engage in the ultimatum game of deal or no deal, and behave regardless of the reality that the deal may not be good; it only has to *feel* good.

Even though we are no longer kids in the checkout line asking for candy, we are still acting on emotional impulses and playing the ultimatum game. The want or need arises emotionally, subconsciously creating a goal which emotionally motivates us, and as we get closer to the goal we experience more emotional feedback; all the while, behavior is subservient. As required by Dad Law, I am very practiced in explaining to children the difference between a want (something you emotionally desire) and a need (something essential to your survival). Children do not see the distinction; in reality, most adults do not either. Why? Because the emotional end goal is the same. We blur the lines because, emotionally, a want and a need are identical to us. Things that make us happy become wants and needs whether the emotional payoff is short or long. How we explain our behavior is where the post-rationalization comes in. We are very good at defending or justifying behavior. The rational facts that were not part of the decision become the evidence as to why we behaved the way we did.

In the case of my ski boot purchase, the offer or price was certainly fair in my mind. I will tell you I got a good deal, but did I? Honestly, I do not know. Seeing the boots triggered the emotions of a want and need, and I became motivated and placed them in my cart. I did not compare prices. I did not visit several sites and grab a pad of paper to create a comparison grid. At that moment, they were the right brand, color, and size, at an acceptable price point, and able to be delivered to my door before Christmas. All of that information was subconsciously processed in milliseconds. It was, from my perspective, a fair deal, and I behaved according to that emotional construct, which in turn culminated with emotional satisfaction. I did not need the boots, but I did want and desire them. I became motivated as I flipped through the boots section and subconsciously goal-oriented to satiate that emotional want.

There is a great deal of science behind the emotional value of "retail therapy." When we go shopping with no *mens rea* to buy something, if we see something that triggers that emotional spark, the positive emotions we feel after acquiring that item are only magnified when we can tell someone what a great deal we got. Affirmation of the deal by others increases the positive emotional feedback and we become more confident in our account of why we behaved the way that we did. Social affirmation is a very powerful motivator of behavior. We want and need to be accepted by our peers. As silly as it may sound, a good deal encapsulates both emotional and social motivators, and we behave in response to these motivations without a scintilla of rational thought.

A recent MIT study revealed that using credit cards stimulates the brain's reward system and an urge for further spending. Credit card shopping increases the motivation to buy and leads to positive emotional feedback, which in turn strengthens the motivation, thereby reinforcing the goal. We feel good when we use a credit card. The study used an fMRI to see the brain activity when people purchased an item with cash or a credit card. Participants were shown various items on a screen, from video games to beauty products, that they could add to their shopping cart. They had the option to pay for the products with cash or a credit card. People were more willing to buy more expensive items with credit than cash and spent more overall when using a credit card. When people bought items with a credit card, the fMRI showed that the striatum, a reward region of the brain, was activated. The striatum is responsible for releasing dopamine and is involved in feelings of reward, positive reinforcement, and feeling pleasure. Paying in cash did not activate the reward networks. Credit cards take advantage of the cognitive biases and emotional mechanisms that enable us to feel good now and postpone feeling bad, giving us more time to post-rationalize why we needed to make the purchase and why it was the rational, right thing to do.

What is fascinating about this study is that it demonstrates how our payment methods have the potential to take advantage of the emotional, neurobiological processes that reinforce and drive purchase behavior. The emotional impetus to buy the product may not be the sole motivator of the purchase behavior, but, combined with the method of payment, the positive emotional feedback accelerates and reinforces the behavior. The credit card payment option tips the positive emotional scale in favor of purchasing.

I Love You, But...

Researchers Emily Garbinsky et al. carried out an interesting behavioral study on the impact of financial infidelity on relationships, quantifying this impact on a Financial Infidelity Scale (FI-Scale). The FI-Scale has strong psychometric properties and predicts financial infidelity among consumers in a relationship; more importantly, it predicts a broad range of consumption-related behaviors that occur despite anticipated partner disapproval.

Much like people involved in the ultimatum game, the individuals the authors studied engaged in a tradeoff where the decisions being made could be financially positive or negative, and in which the behaviors that occur are primed by emotion. In this scenario, however, there is an additional element of emotion added: the relationship of the couple. It is thus a higher stakes ultimatum game. One person in the relationship was placed in a scenario where they could make a purchase, even though that purchase would negatively impact the relationship. They were then provided with behaviors to avoid the negative impact through deceit. The measurement Garbinsky et al. sought to make is at what point did the participants engage in deceit to avoid the potential perceived negative repercussions?

One of the measurement points was the monetary threshold of when a partner should be consulted on a purchase. At what dollar amount is a spending behavior an acceptable deal, a fair offer that requires no disclosure? Unsurprisingly, there is a considerable disparity in what various individuals deem to be fair and acceptable. The gap occurs across gender, age, income, and a host of other demographic metrics. Our perception of what is fair and unfair is relative to a host of social and economic factors as well. On average, in the United States, a purchase would need to rise to $400 to be considered an expense worth discussing with a partner. Luckily for me, the amount goes up with age, and I am pretty sure there is a Grateful Dead concert addiction exclusion. We are all walking around with a number that represents the amount at or above which we would feel we should disclose a purchase.

What is interesting in the financial infidelity study is that while the decision to accept the offer to avoid disclosing the purchase is emotionally based, just as in the ultimatum game, it is positive emotionally to the decision maker but often not to the relationship of the couple. Despite the potential negative impact on the relationship, the personal emotional payoff drove behavior, up to a particular threshold. If I wanted $200 tickets, I could happily buy them and feel giddy that I was going to the show. I am confident that I do not need to disclose this purchase, and even if I did the outcome would be positive. However, if I bought $400 tickets, I would still feel the positive emotions up to the point of purchase, but because I had crossed the disclosure threshold, the potential for negative feedback could lead to deceptive behavior to avoid the negative emotions. I may now not disclose the purchase or may "discount" the price to show I got a good deal. Either way, the likelihood of my engaging in financial infidelity has greatly increased. Even though I know before I click "buy" on those $400 tickets that there will be negative emotional consequences, I will click "buy," and I will do so because I am emotionally motivated, despite the possible consequences. I will engage in deceptive behavior that probabilistically only increases the magnitude of negative emotional consequences. This study accentuates how powerful the emotional pathway is in producing behavior outside of any rational cognitive thought. So be sure to throw away your ticket stub before you leave the show!

In this next section we are going to investigate how our emotional construct operates at a subconscious level, influencing and directing our behaviors like an invisible hand. Our emotions direct when we focus our attention and what we pay attention to. Emotion shapes what we remember and what we think we remember. We will examine how our visual world is directly processed into emotion, guiding us to behave. We will analyze how emotions can direct behavior without any conscious realization of an emotional experience. Lastly, we will delve into how the emotions of others can become our own and influence what we do, even if we have not directly experienced what caused the emotion.

Chapter Four:
Subconscious Emotional
Influences

May I Feel Your Attention

Emotion strongly influences our attention, modulating the level of attention as well as motivating action and behavior. When emotionally engaged we can be more in tune or less in tune with surrounding factors that, absent the emotional stimuli, would provoke cognitive thought, resulting in different behavior. We can become emotionally "blinded" in that our attention becomes hyper-focused on how we feel, and our rational cognitive pathway is closed or impaired.

The attentional and executive control of emotion is also linked to our learning processes, as intrinsically limited attentional capacities impact our focus on relevant information. As already discussed, emotion also facilitates encoding of memories and greatly impacts the retrieval of information. We will remember how we feel more than we will the surrounding facts that caused the emotion. We process and prioritize emotional information more readily, and it is core to our behavioral response.

More specifically, emotion regulates the allocation of processing resources and determines our behavior by tuning us to the world in certain biased ways, thus steering us toward things that "feel good" while avoiding things that "feel bad." This indicates that emotion guides behavior and motivates desires according to unique goal orientation.

Because we do not have the capacity to simultaneously process everything, we have separate attentional mechanisms which correspond to our System 1 and System 2 pathways. System 1 attentional processing assesses the emotional situation—is it positive or negative?—and draws upon the appropriate memory patterns to choose how to behave and to encode the information. We emotionally assess quickly, involuntarily, and subconsciously and behave in our best emotional interest. The System 2 attention mechanism requires concentration to construct thoughts in an orderly series of steps. This type of attention is necessary to problem solve. Experimental studies have examined the phenomenon of increased System 1 attention when individuals are emotionally stimulated by using various attentional tasks. These investigations demonstrated a bias in attentional processing toward emotionally stimulating content, followed by an increase in emotional responses. Moreover, one study compared healthy subjects with a group of patients with bilateral amygdala damage, like that experienced by the patients of Dr. Damasio. The results revealed that the healthy subjects exhibited increased perception of and attention toward emotional words compared to the patients, indicating that the amygdala plays a crucial role in emotional processing. In addition, functional neuroimaging showed that the brain regions that regulate attentional focus by integrating external and internal inputs create emotional feedback. Increased attention due to emotional feedback in turn engages our motivation.

Ponder for a moment that when you hear a story, listen to a speaker, or read a book, the more emotive the subject or the speaker is, the more engaged we are with the content. If there is an emotional connection to the content or the passion in the speaker's voice, we feel engaged and our level of attention increases. Mundane events or topics are not only forgotten easily, we are not motivated by them. If I showed you a video of a person standing on a sidewalk for thirty seconds, there would be little to no reaction and little recall of what happened. However, if I showed you a video of a person in a field laughing and rolling and being chased by corgi puppies, there would be an emotional reaction and you would recall most if not all of the details. The emotional tone or setting engages our emotional attention. We can feel the happiness of the person laughing and being chased by those puppies. We may smile or even laugh while watching it. Emotional content not only triggers an emotional response, it also increases the amount of passive information we are processing. We become emotional sponges because we prioritize emotional information.

Early in my consumer research career, I was charged with testing TV advertising utilizing a method that created an awareness score. While the algorithm was a company secret, the components were not. I tested hundreds of TV ads, and the analysis was simple and formulaic. To be more engaging, an advertisement needed an emotional tone. It could be funny, sad, or even outrageous. If there was no emotional tonality, consumers would not pay attention and the ad would test poorly. Humor was a double-edged sword, as not everyone gets the joke, or it may offend. When an ad used what I called puppies and babies emotions, it would always produce a winning score. In short, if the ad was emotionally relatable and left viewers with that tug at the heart, it was a winner. I was fortunate enough to be involved in the brilliant, 20-year-plus McCann-Erickson "Priceless" campaign for MasterCard. The ad formula itself became a branding device. The voiceover would narrate a purchase of an item at some price point, then a second item at a second price point; the third narration would creatively show how those items created a "priceless" moment—the intangible emotional payoff. The ads were all about creating a connection to that emotional, "priceless" moment. Consumers paid attention and the campaign created an immense amount of emotional equity for the brand and drove behavior. The emotional relevance of the stimulus was prioritized and influenced attention.

We have a heightened awareness of emotional tonality, and we prioritize that information. We do so even if it slows our ability to make a decision or to behave. We find an emotionally good decision preferable to a rationally good decision. This prioritization of emotional information can directly impact our perceptions by increasing our emotional sensitivity. We become so focused on the emotion that we can block out other factors and stimuli and become more emotionally aware ourselves. The emotional processing not only enriches our experiences with emotions, but it can also directly shape the content of our perceptions and awareness. We believe what we feel, we see what we feel. Most importantly, these effects arise involuntarily.

Memory, Attention, and the Law

Well before I became involved in behavioral science and its application to consumer marketing, I was a trial attorney. As part of my study in criminal law we explored the impact of emotion on attention and memory, from two different perspectives. The first was the impact of emotion on our ability to recollect details surrounding an event. The goal was to demonstrate that an emotionally charged event created vivid memories in witnesses, but details were often not recalled or supplanted by false details. We also explored how emotional priming can create a pathway to inject "facts" that did not exist. This training was to expose us to the flaws of witness memory and confessions.

Law school is taught by the Socratic method; there are no lectures, but rather intense discussions that the professor leads to draw out the learnings from the students. It is a rather nebulous experience, one of not knowing whether you understand because there are no answers—only more questions. The classroom is set up as a multi-tiered semi-circle, with four aisles dividing it so that the professor can wander among the students. As part of criminal law class, the professor, unbeknownst to the students, would stage a robbery. The robbery was very realistic: a person came into the room, had a brief confrontation, and ran off with a laptop or bag. In my class, it was so real to us that a few people chased the suspect down the hall into the parking lot. We then spent weeks collectively building factual memories of what had happened. In the end, we proved how impactful emotion was, and not only on our personal memory; when we tried to create a collective memory, more facts were lost, and more details arose that never occurred. We were thinking after the emotionally charged behavior. It was through the use of this post-rationalized thought process that we filled in the story with "cognitive facts": things that must be true in order for the sequence of events to have occurred. As we worked through those facts, they became "truer" and more intertwined with the emotion. As young lawyers do, we would argue the truth of these "facts" with passionate monologues, only to see our flaws exposed when the video tape was given to us. We were wrong on a lot of the details—things we were absolutely certain of.

As consumers, when we behave subject to our emotions, the memory of why we behaved the way we did is subject to a post-rationalized filling in of facts. I will tell you that I bought those ski boots because of all of their features and benefits, some of which I read about only when the box was in my hand on Christmas Day. I had to read the manual to understand the adjustable canting feature and walk mode, but I know when I showcased those new boots to my ski buddies these were top features: features that I did not consider when purchasing and did not know I "needed." The final absurdity is that I adjusted the canting one time, and I have never used walk mode. So, while emotion is important to memory formation, it can cause us to remember the emotion over the details. When we try to understand the details or explain to others why we acted as we did, we systematically and unconsciously pull in details to show rational thought that never occurred. What we think we did and the process we went through to arrive at that decision or behavior is inherently misrepresented by our emotional construct. We explain away our emotional behavior because society demands rational decisions. One of my favorite statements of Daniel Kahneman's is "We think far less than we think we do."

After law school, one of my jobs was picking juries for trials. Depending on which side of the case you are on, emotion or the absence of it is a powerful tool. One side wants a juror who is fully System 2: slow, controlled, rule-following, conscious-thinking. The other side wants a juror who is System 1: emotional, associative, fast, involuntary. I tended to be on the lookout for the System 1 juror. Trials are not as glamorous as they appear on TV; they are more like a chess game. As part of the jury selection process, each potential juror fills out a short questionnaire with some basic background information: occupation, relationships with law enforcement or medical fields, any reasons why they cannot be on the jury. The prospective jurors are questioned in a process called *voir dire*, where both attorneys can ask questions and put forth an argument to the judge as to why this juror should not be on the jury or should be accepted. I would go through the questionnaires and immediately eliminate any jurors connected to the medical or law enforcement fields. Next, I would look for professions that required math or detail-orientated processes. I would focus on professions that fit my case, professions that I could relate somehow to the case, but they needed to be jobs that required emotion-based or gut-based decisions. I wanted people who were street smart, not book smart.

As part of the *voir dire* process, my goal was to plant a seed of emotional connection, either to my client, to the case, or to me. As the case would unfold, I would draw upon these emotional connections to solidify memories and to focus attention toward or away from facts. I would systematically create a series of emotional connections with each juror that would be used in the final arguments. An amazing aspect of emotion is that we can conjure up a memory and feel the associated emotion, not just subjectively but physiologically; we can create the neural activity that produces the emotion. The goal of a trial attorney is to get the jury to feel the emotions of the case: to tell a story that actually elicits an emotional response, which in turn will result in the desired behavior. Creating memories in the jurors' minds and capturing or diverting attention also require emotion. Juror behavior was far more malleable when emotions could be connected to an outcome. What we believe to be true and what captures our attention depends on the strength of the emotions surrounding the event. In the end, we want to feel that we made the right decision, not decide rationally that we did. I was a law clerk for a criminal court judge for a period of time and would often interact with the jury after a case. I would always ask jurors about their decision, and the response was always that they *felt* like it was the right decision.

Feeling What We See

We process and respond to visual information faster and more efficiently than any other type of information. With ninety percent of the information transmitted to the brain being visual, it is important to understand the role emotion plays in the interpretation of that visual information.

Several neuroimaging studies show that emotional activity in the amygdala correlates with enhanced responses to emotional stimuli in the visual cortex. More direct evidence comes from recent fMRI results among patients such as Dr. Damasio's, which show that amygdala damage can prevent visual activation for emotional stimuli. Patients without the ability to feel emotions cannot be visually stimulated to divert attention to emotional stimuli or feel a corresponding emotion. They are emotionally blind, in all senses of the word.

Anatomical tracing studies show that the amygdala not only receives inputs from visual pathways, but also sends connections back to virtually all processing stages along the visual system, including the primary visual cortex. We feel what we see, and we do so at a lightning-fast implicit rate. During this process, we create an "attentional blink" where what we feel about an item of visual information is prioritized to impact behavior.

Visual stimuli trigger an appraisal of emotional significance or emotional categorization more quickly than the more elaborate and prolonged cortical processing associated with conscious awareness. Let us break this response process down into its three parts. First, our emotional system reacts to visual stimuli before the visual information can be processed to identify what the visual is. Second, the emotional system has already determined if the visual is emotionally positive or negative before we can cognitively process what the visual is. Lastly, our emotional system has a primed behavioral response at the ready once we cognitively affirm the visual.

The nature of this visual response mechanism goes back to the previous discussion of human face recognition and the work by Dr. Paul Ekman. We are not only "fast seeing" but also "fast feeling" the visual world around us. This ability to emotionally respond to visual stimuli through a subconscious process is the basis of the field of visual semiotics. Visual semiotics is the analysis of the subconscious emotions and messages visual images communicate through signs and symbols that we feel and see. I will dig deeper into this System 1 passive approach later.

Our brain operates more than ninety percent on visual information, and other information is "visualized" to speed its integration. A recent MIT study reveals that not only is ninety percent of information transmitted to our brain visually, but the human brain processes images in 13 milliseconds, 60,000 times faster than it processes text and about 700 milliseconds before our conscious brain can recognize stimuli.

The average person is exposed to over 10,000 image-based impressions a day. That is a minimum of 1.5 million data points processed unconsciously. By contrast, the average person takes in fewer than a thousand words and a dozen numeric comparisons per day. We receive thousands of times more visual data impressions than any other type of information. This balance of information types is consistent with how our System 1 pathway accounts for ninety-five percent of our behavior, while System 2 accounts for the remaining five percent. The visual structure of our environment informs our emotional construct to allow us to subconsciously "fast see" and "fast feel" so that we can behave without overwhelming our System 2 pathway.

Now take this "feel what we see" construct into the realm of marketing and advertising. Packaging needs to command attention visually. If it did not, there would be a lot of black and white boxes on shelves, and their appearance would not matter. Our visual attention is first and foremost going to be an emotional assessment. How a consumer feels is going to be determined by six semiotic structures: color, shape, physical context, social context, responsibility, and experiential context. We are not going to choose a package that evokes negative emotions. We are not going to choose a package that is out of the emotional context of what we want or need. We choose packages that are emotionally appealing. Our System 2 self will tell us we chose a package because of what is inside or the objective images on the package as a whole. However, how we feel about the package has already happened; it happened before we cognitively registered what the artwork was on the package. Our attention has blinked, having assessed whether the package emotionally delivers on our subconscious goal, and most of the time we already have that package in our hand or in the cart without any rational thought.

Feeling Without Knowing

To say that we are conscious of our own emotions sounds like a truism. After all, emotions are feelings, so how could we have feelings that are not felt? Of course, we sometimes may not know what caused our emotion or may not know why we feel a particular emotion, as when we feel anxious for what seems no particular reason. On occasion, we may even incorrectly construe our own emotional state, such as when we angrily deny that we are angry. We presume that the emotion itself is intrinsically conscious and that, with attention, it can be brought into the full light of awareness.

With this view, we believe that conscious feelings are a central and necessary ingredient of an emotional reaction. However, emotion can also be genuinely unconscious. We can have both positive and negative emotional reactions that are inaccessible to introspection. Despite the absence of subjective feelings, unconscious emotional reactions can influence people's preference judgments and their corresponding behavior.

We can define two paths for emotion: implicit (occurring without attention or intention) and explicit. An explicit emotion refers to a person's conscious awareness of an emotion, feeling, or mood state; implicit emotion refers to changes in experience, thought, actions or behaviors that are attributable to a person's emotional state, independent of his or her conscious awareness of that state. Over the past two decades, evidence that the human amygdala exerts some of its functions when the person is not aware of the content, or even presence, of the triggering emotional stimulus has accumulated.

The amygdala operates at the intersection of conscious and non-conscious emotional processing. These two different modes of processing incoming sensory information co-exist in the brain, allocating subconsciousness System 1 attention and conscious System 2 attention. Investigations have shown consistently that non-conscious emotional stimuli elicit activity in the amygdala, which aligns with corresponding activity in the brain's visual pathways. We can both see what we feel and feel what we see.

In fact, studies on patients with cortical blindness provide the best characterization of non-conscious perception of emotions. These patients can discriminate the emotional content of stimuli that they cannot see consciously—a phenomenon known as affective blindsight—and their proficiency is associated with activity in the amygdala. We can feel without any visual confirmation of the stimuli: feeling without seeing.

We have two subconscious paths: without visual information through a subcortical route and with visual information through a cortical route, both with the ability to convey information to the amygdala and sustain non-conscious emotion processing.

The neural networks for conscious and non-conscious emotion processing are not entirely segregated. The amygdala not only contributes to both modes of processing, but its initial response without awareness helps to determine whether the stimulus will reach awareness and how it will modulate behavioral and bodily reactions. Our emotional system processes how we feel, and based upon our positive or negative feelings our behavior is already queued up; then, and only if appropriate, our emotional system informs our cognitive awareness. If our emotional system assesses positive or neutral emotions, it carries on to create an emotional goal, motivation and behavior that aids in achieving that emotional positivity or maintaining neutrality. When we process negative feelings, our behavior, depending on the level of negative emotions, can be queued up and occur automatically, such as in the case of a fear reaction, or our emotional system pulls in our cognitive attention to focus on the stimuli and determine with more acuity our response.

At some point in my career, I was involved in an executive training program. Part of the program was the assessment of nonverbal cues or habits that we all demonstrate that signal how we feel in a particular work scenario. I am not, nor could I be, a good poker player. I apparently telegraph in very obvious ways my disagreement. While this was advantageous as a trial attorney, it is not good practice outside of the courtroom. One of the takeaways was that crossing my arms signals that I am not open to what is being said. I am now very aware of this visual cue and the emotional perception that accompanies it. When I cross my arms, the speaker's non-conscious response to this emotional stimulus could be to pause and question me directly; proceed, aware that I am not in agreement; ignore me altogether; or prevent me from expressing my disagreement. The speaker's emotional assessment is that I am a "threat" to their point of view. They are prepared behaviorally to treat me as a threat even if I am not one. I may fully agree with their point, but that is not the feeling I am invoking subconsciously through my body language. The visual information is processed by the emotional construct as negative, and the speaker prepares to respond behaviorally in such a way as to avoid the negative emotion or confront it. The emotion is in the room even if the speaker is not conscious of the assessment.

While non-conscious perception of emotional stimuli induces behavior, these behavioral outcomes are quantitatively and qualitatively different from those occurring during conscious emotion perception. Behavior that occurs tends to be stronger and more immediate when awareness is lacking. This suggests that non-conscious perception of emotional stimuli is not simply a degraded version of conscious perception, but a different mode of processing the same stimuli. We can feel different degrees of emotion depending on how the emotion is processed and then behave in different ways. For example, emotional stimuli that prompt a non-conscious response can interfere with our ability to complete a task. We become emotionally engaged in a way that delays or disengages our attention, which results in behavior that may have been different if we had had more information before behaving.

We instantaneously synchronize our facial expressions with the emotional meaning of other individuals' expressions. The behavior occurs quickly, without awareness, and the facial expression is quickly associated with and communicates a corresponding emotion. We are in fact exchanging subconscious emotional signals that both impact and cause behavior in social interactions.

We can experience consciously the behaviors and emotions caused by an unseen and unperceived emotional stimulus only when we link them to the conscious representations of their external causes (e.g., an angry expression or a sudden noise). In fact, we are unable to report a conscious feeling despite the fact that, at the same time, our behavior reveals the presence of an emotional reaction triggered by exposure to an external stimulus of which we are unaware. We can feel and behave subconsciously and only become cognizant if we can formulate a conscious cause: in other words, a post-rationalized thought or reason. The cause or reason for why we felt an emotion and behaved in a particular way must present itself to the conscious mind before we can connect them. Most of the time we do not formulate that conscious cause because we do not need to. However, when we do, we may not even "know" what the external cause was, so we fill in the blanks with things that make logical sense to us.

My affinity to Crest toothpaste and decades of purchase behavior had never been brought to the forefront of rational thought until my wife questioned me that fateful morning in 1996, immediately triggering a search for logical causes that would support my behavior: nine out of ten dentists recommend it, fluoride, whitening, decay and gingivitis prevention, and every other factual attribute or statement I could bring into the discussion. I certainly could not say, I do not know why! I had somehow convinced her to marry me under the guise that I possessed a certain amount of intelligence and could not now come clean with the admission that I engaged in no cognition regarding a simple behavior. Yet, much to her dismay, I had been purchasing Crest toothpaste with no conscious cause and had been doing it for a very long time. There was a relationship between my emotion and my resulting behavior, one that existed outside of cognitive thought.

An emotional process may remain entirely unconscious, even when we are attentive and motivated to describe our feelings correctly. Such an emotional process may nevertheless drive our behavior and physiological reactions, even while remaining inaccessible to conscious awareness. A great deal of advertising and marketing focus has been placed on subliminally induced emotional reactions. One body of work focusing on consumption behaviors or preference judgments demonstrated that people can be influenced by emotional visual stimuli and yet subjectively feel unchanged.

In studies by Winkielman, Piotr, and Berridge, subjects were subliminally presented emotional stimuli to promote an emotional reaction, and after the exposure they consumed a beverage. The subjects' emotional state was assessed throughout the process. The findings were that subliminally presented emotional stimuli can cause emotional reactions that alter consumption behavior without eliciting conscious feelings at the moment the emotional reactions are caused. The results demonstrated that unconscious emotional impact is powerful enough to alter behavior and that people are simply not aware of either the emotion or the behavioral impact, even when presented with the process.

The power of this unconscious emotion may sound like science fiction or something out of the CIA playbook, but if we break the process down, it is very observable. When we are feeling positive emotions or are consciously in a good mood, we behave in a very different way than if we are feeling negative emotions or are in a bad mood. What we consume or buy can vary greatly depending on how we feel. As a result of the creation of positive emotions, even if they are implicit, we behave differently. While we may not be consciously aware that we are in a positive state, or of what caused that positive state, we will behave differently than if we were in a negative state. If our mind associates the positive feeling with the behavior, it creates the connective tissue of the goal-motivation-emotional feedback loop. In these tests, positive emotional states led not only to more consumption but to an increase in "liking." When we are in a positive emotional state, we feel good, and we want to stay in a positive emotional position, so we are more open to and outwardly display positive affinity. We can have subliminally triggered emotional reactions that drive judgment and behavior even in the absence of any conscious feelings accompanying these reactions. Our unconscious emotions are connected to the subcortical brain systems that underlie basic "liking" reactions.

A dramatic demonstration of this point comes from emotion-based neuroscience studies with anencephalic human infants. The brain of such infants is congenitally malformed; they possess only a brain stem and lack nearly all structures at the top or front of the brain, including the entire cortex. Yet sweet tastes of sugar still elicit positive facial expressions of pleasure from anencephalic infants, whereas bitter tastes elicit negative facial expressions of disgust. The basic premise is positivity creates positivity. An experience (e.g., drinking a new beverage) in a positive emotional state is going to be associated with that positive emotional state. We will pursue or change our behavior to maintain that positivity. We can lack consciousness not only of the causes of the emotion, but also of our own emotional reaction itself— even if that emotional reaction is intense enough to alter our behavior.

Feeling What Others Feel

Have you ever been part of a conversation where someone is telling a funny story, and the storyteller and some people in the group start laughing, and then you are laughing even though you did not get the joke, or it was not really that funny? Maybe the cashier at the coffee shop smiles at you and for some reason you not only smile back but walk out of the shop with a halo of positivity. As part of our social interaction with other people, we are not only acutely aware through visual cues how others feel, but we tend to feel the emotions of others through emotional mimicry. We subconsciously process the emotions in the room and align ourselves with those emotions, even though we are far removed from the stimulus that caused the emotion.

It makes sense that on a basic level a group of people who are emotionally aligned are socially a tighter group and that the aligned emotional tone provides an advantage for the group in working towards or against the behaviors that will sustain or change the emotional tenor. Having members of the group on the same emotional plane allows for improved communications and decision making. This underlying mechanism of emotional mimicry exists not only with visual stimuli, such as faces; we can subconsciously assemble emotional tone with sounds, gestures, and other behaviors that are not as direct as a smile. Emotional mimicry is often associated with the word contagion: the spread and communication of an emotion among a group in close contact. We impact others with our emotions in a way that is a subconscious contagion. I am tired or bored and yawn; slowly, that yawn will spread through the group. This shared emotion can then impact how we behave. We may leave the boring setting, go home for the night, have a cup of coffee, ask the waiter for the check. The yawn is a signal to the group that a change agent is needed because attention is lost; we feel bored or tired. The ability to understand and share the feelings of another is also known as empathy. When we are empathetic, we behave differently than if we were to experience the same emotion in isolation. The social factors keep us in a state of emotional alignment.

The occurrence and functions of emotional mimicry can be explained from a social contextual perspective. Emotional mimicry serves an affiliation function and occurs when an emotional signal is perceived and promotes social bonds and mutual understanding. The strength of emotional mimicry and its impact depends on the relationship between the expresser and the observer because the interpretation of an emotional signal also depends on how one relates to the expresser. For example, a positive view of the expresser, a cooperative social context, or the expresser being a social ingroup member have all been shown to elicit more mimicry. We mimic the emotions of people who are close to us, people we hold in high regard, and people we want to be like. We have empathy for the people we surround ourselves with and those we aspire to be with.

Both mimicry and the contagion effects in people occur without any conscious awareness or control on the part of the individuals involved. The perception of an emotional expression and the processing of that emotional expression entail the reactivation of the neural states that are involved in their production. When we perceive an emotion, we reproduce that feeling neurologically. In fact, observers of people experiencing different emotions utilize the identical neural processes activated during the experience of these emotions. We feel what others feel just by observing emotional reactions, even though we have not interacted with the cause of the emotion. Human experiments with single neuron recordings have revealed that the observation of pain and its experience activate the same neurons.

We biologically feel and recreate the emotions experienced by others in our mind. We do not just have an abstract sympathetic response; we process and feel the emotion using the same neural structures and processes that would be employed if we were to experience the emotion independently. Emotional mimicry is so powerful that our body causes us to feel, quite literally, what others are feeling. Ponder for a moment how a subconscious change in your emotional state could impact your behavior even when the emotion was not your own to begin with.

Studies have shown that by artificially inducing or constricting facial expressions associated with emotions, people can influence and change the behaviors of others. Mimicry and facial feedback both demonstrate that an observer's judgement of an unknown stimulus can be impacted. This formulation focuses on a social-influence process driven by the emotional empathy between the producer of the initial emotion and the perceiver. If the perceiver sees and feels positive emotions, they adopt those positive emotions even though they have not assessed the stimuli independently.

A simple example that anyone can relate to is people's response when a food product, such as milk, is bad. A person smells the milk or has a sip and there is a visceral reaction of disgust. Yet what happens? They want you to affirm it is indeed bad. This is my job in our household: royal taste tester for spoiled food. Even if the milk is perfectly fine, you are emotionally primed for a bad experience. You may be so emotionally aligned that you will not even try the milk, let alone smell it. In fact, you may physically start to react just thinking about the taste, even if you have not made the assessment yourself. The emotional reaction of others can become our own emotional perceptions and affect our behavior without any experience ourselves of the stimuli that caused the primary emotional reaction.

The phenomena of emotional mimicry and contagions have been studied using canned laughter and by placing smiling subjects into discussions about topics that would not regularly produce a positive emotion. Hearing canned laughter and seeing someone smiling both induce an involuntary facial muscle reaction in a perceiver, and this in turn induces not only a reciprocal physical response (feeling a positive emotion and smiling back), but also a positive evaluative response to the stimuli. A control to this body of work is the study of individuals with autism spectrum disorders who do not show spontaneous emotional mimicry. These patients demonstrate an impairment in understanding other people's emotional states. The inability both to perceive the emotions of other people and to physically mimic their emotional response to stimuli impairs their evaluative response. In short, without an emotional context, they cannot formulate a decision or behavior. This corresponds to the findings of the work previously discussed involving Dr. Klin's patient Peter and Dr. Damasio's patient Elliot.

Emotional mimicry as both a contagion and as part of our social empathy impacts not only our judgment but also our behavior. This emotional lever has been exploited by TV with canned laughter, which tells us when we should laugh and that the content was funny. It is also used in advertising in which smiling and laughing subjects are shown interacting with a product, conveying the positive emotions we want to feel and that we may actually feel in that moment while watching the ad. Pharma ads utilize this behavioral science technique to deflect and override the negative emotions associated with the disease, showing smiling faces and happy interactions and showcasing emotionally what is possible with this new drug, all while the narrator is going on about the side effects, including death. Emotional mimicry is at the heart of marketing and advertising; products are portrayed in an emotionally positive social setting, planting the seed of connectivity between the emotion felt and portrayed and the product itself. The different types of emotions we feel in response to stimuli such as advertising emerge from a construction process. That is, basic psychological operations, such as perception, attention, and memory, combine to generate an emotional meaning that is influenced by the social factors which are core to emotional empathy and mimicry.

At this point you may be realizing that we are emotional beings that can think, and you would be right. Our emotional construct is behind the scenes in the subconscious mind, guiding our behavior in such a way that to our conscious mind we "think" we made a System 2 rational decision when in reality we have not. In the next section we will delve into how our System 1 pathway makes decisions with imperfect or incomplete information using fast, associative and pattern-seeking mechanisms. We will examine two forms of System 1 decision mechanisms:

biases and heuristics. We will also evaluate how these mechanisms contribute to the post-rationalization narrative that consumers create to explain their behavior.

Chapter Five:
System 1 Biases and Heuristics

Are We Good at Making System 1 Decisions?

At the outset I put forth that the pathway to human decision making is that we feel, behave, and lastly think. By understanding this pathway, people in charge of brands, marketing, and insights can gain a holistic view of the decision process and utilize that understanding to their advantage. To understand the decision pathway, we began broadly with Daniel Kahneman's two systems of thinking: System 1, the unconscious, fast, associative, involuntary, emotion-based system that processes and controls 95% of our decision making; and System 2, the conscious, rule-following, slow, controlled, rational-based system that is responsible for the remaining 5% of our decisions. We tend to think that we are rational human beings who think about our decisions and behaviors. However, we are (almost) completely irrational. Why? Because our emotion-based decision system is our evolutionary survival mechanism.

We then explored the symbiotic relationship between System 1 and System 2 and the brain's deference to System 1 decision making—more importantly, what happens when our System 1 decisions are challenged or we need to explain those decisions to others, and the resulting rationalized thinking that occurs after the decision and behavior. We examined how we try to explain why we reached a decision through a rational lens when the decision and behavior occurred completely subconsciously; we honestly do not consciously know why we behaved the way we did.

This disconnect is the Achilles heel for people charged with consumer insights, marketing, and brands who want to know what people "think": believing not only that consumer decisions are rationally based, but that consumers can explain them. Consumers' decisions are based not on what they think, but on what they feel.

To understand the System 1 pathway, we deeply explored the role of emotion in behavior and decision making, the inability to make decisions without an emotional construct, and how emotions subconsciously act through mechanisms such as attention, memory, motivation, and goals. We also discussed the subconscious influence of feeling what we see, feeling without awareness, and feeling what others feel, all of which dictate our behavior and decisions. Our emotions are the gateway to our decision making and resulting behavior.

Are we effective at making emotion-based System 1 decisions? The answer is yes we are effective at making System 1 decisions, but are they good decisions? Part of Daniel Kahneman's work and research by others is the notion that, given the same inputs, the two thought systems arrive at different results. When we are forced into a System 2 mode of thinking, we will not make the same decision. We explored this concept with the ultimatum game, which, if played within a System 2 mindset, aligns with rational economic theory: both players would profit, and every offer would be accepted. We have all taken an exam and gone back and changed an answer only to find out that our first, instinctual answer was correct. We begin to give importance to factors that are not part of the solution and to create contingent scenarios that lead either to analysis paralysis or confirmation basis.

Researchers at Cornell University estimate we make 226.7 decisions each day on food alone. The average adult is estimated to make about 35,000 decisions each day. Each one of those decisions, of course, carries certain emotional consequences that are both good and bad. Our daily decisions differ in difficulty and in importance: from what morning beverage you choose to where you park your car, which email you read first, and so on. However, they all must be made every day. This is why we sleep for a quarter of the day. If we had to consciously process all these decisions, our brain would crash. Our automatic System 1 takes on those decisions and protects our System 2, preventing cognitive overload. System 1 processes this torrent of inputs through neural shortcuts, which Kahneman calls heuristics. A heuristic is a flexible problem-solving method that uses shortcuts to produce good-enough solutions for quick decisions. Instead of examining pieces of data individually, we subconsciously compare any new information to associative patterns we have already formed. The key here is that the solution does not need to be optimal, perfect, logical, or rational—just sufficient for reaching an immediate goal. This is where emotional motivation and the subconscious goal cycle play a dominant role. We do not need to make the best decision; we just need a decision that feels right and optimizes that positive emotive balance.

The way we create heuristics is by assessing the information at hand and connecting that information to our experience. Heuristics are strategies derived from previous experiences with similar problems. Our experience is also a memory, and as we have previously discussed, emotions play a dominant role in not only what we remember, but how we remember it. Our experience is also more than cause and effect; it incorporates the social context of each experience, the emotional outcome, and expected outcomes of social norms. Our core heuristic is to subconsciously compare any new information with associative emotional patterns we have already formed.

The availability of a heuristic provides us with a mental shortcut. This shortcut relies on memories of experiences that immediately come to a person's mind. We value information that springs to mind quickly as being more significant. Again, this is why emotion is a critical component of what we remember and how we remember it. When we make a decision, we automatically compare and contrast our current situation to related events or situations, not rationally but emotionally. We remember how the previous experiences made us feel and then assess the decision based on whether that emotion was beneficial. There is a downside to heuristics: they are often influenced by biases, and they are often logically flawed or wrong. This is not surprising, since they are nothing more than shortcuts that usually involve focusing on one aspect of a complex problem and ignoring others. Therefore, heuristics affect our decision-making and our behavior.

Cognitive Biases

We all suffer from and rely on cognitive biases. A cognitive bias is a systematic pattern of deviation from a social norm or from rationality in judgment whereby inferences about other people and situations may be drawn in an illogical fashion. As individuals we create our own subjective social reality from our own perception of any input. We implicitly believe things to be true even though they are not true; the strength of our association or belief overrides rational logic. An example I often use about the strength of implicit beliefs (and one that ages me) is the association of safety with Volvo. Volvos were never the safest cars; they were one of the first cars to feature seat belts, but the beloved boxy tank of a car became the centerpiece of a marketing campaign focused on safety. What else could Volvo do with such a slow, ugly car? Some of us were forced by our parents to drive these cars, and we were so safe that no one wanted to be seen riding with us in one. Safety and Volvo were synonymous even though there was no rational or logical truth to the association, but parents quoted it like fact, and it became implicitly true. Implicit truths are very powerful factors in our application of heuristics.

In marketing and consumer insights we often ignore implicit truths; we are, after all, a very rational and logical group, or so we believe. We ask about features and benefits and future behavior, and we create lovely data charts that have the air of scientific precision, but what we ask of consumers is not only to rationalize a process that was not rational, but to fit it into our own structured box. We provide the answer choices and lead them down the path to explicit data. We want the numbers to an equation that we believe is the path to the answer. However, as in the case of some scientific equations, there are variables that are observable and those that are not, but the impact of the latter on the outcome is ever-present. It is very difficult to overcome an implicit truth, and if you do not know it is even there you may be challenging it unwittingly. Yet appealing to an implicit truth is a catalyst to alignment and behavior. Reinforcing what people already believe, even if it is false, is marketing gold. Yet we often want to correct the implicit truths, or, even worse, ignore them. Innovators see them for what they are: opportunities.

I recently presented some Implicit Association Test (IAT) data to a client. IAT is a behavioral science technique that evolved from the academic discipline of cognitive psychology and is one of the mainstream methods for studying human cognition and emotion. IAT uses reaction time in milliseconds to discriminate subconscious brain processes from conscious thoughts or decisions. This measurement can occur because conscious and subconscious mental processes occur within different timeframes, allowing for insight into the two distinct paths for decision making: System 1, the implicit fast path, and System 2, the explicit slow path. The most well-known and continuous studies are the Harvard IATs, which focus on social biases. IATs come in many formats, each with its own advantages and disadvantages. IAT and the measurement of reaction time in the brain is a very documented tool and process in the cognitive sciences and is often used in conjunction with fMRI scans of the brain, which visualize the brain processes.

The data I was discussing showed that, when asked to choose among a set of movie titles, a majority of consumers (65%) chose A. However, when we looked at the implicit data, the strongest movie title was B (52%). The implicit data for A was only 39%. The kneejerk reaction by the client was, "great: A is the winner." Would you rather be marketing a movie title that consumers subconsciously and emotionally want to see, or would you rather try to appeal to the rational explicit title choice? With the strong implicit title, the desire already exists. Head-to-head, more consumers implicitly chose title B. As a marketer, you still need to appeal to the explicit thinking group; their think time in the decision was slow because there was indecision! When we pause to "think," we do so because something does not fit the pattern heuristic we are tapping into for this decision. This is not to say we will not reach the same decision, but we may not. This is the unknown. What was disheartening was how long it took for the client to grasp that taking advantage of the implicit bias was a good thing. Sometimes it takes speaking to it in the negative: showing how hard it is to convince someone that something they believe is untrue. We do not have to go far in this world of fake news, social media "truths," and trending ideologies to find examples of things that people implicitly and emotionally believe to be true, and one would be hard pressed to convince them otherwise; all of the marketing dollars in the world will not move the needle. In contrast, those who spend with the already existing implicit truth have momentum.

Cognitive Biases in Action

Cognitive biases—or cognitive illusions, as Dr. Daniel Kahneman refers to them—affect our everyday lives and the success of decisions. The first one I would like to explore is attribute substitution. Attribute substitution occurs when an individual must make a judgment (of a target attribute) that is computationally complex and instead substitutes a more easily calculated heuristic attribute.

If someone is asked a complicated question, such as one that involves predicting the probability of an event (will it snow next week?), they cannot answer it because it is very difficult. But there are easier questions that are related to that one that they can answer, such as: Is it cold outside? That is something that people know right away. What happens is people take the answer to the easy question, they use it to answer the difficult question, and they think they have answered the difficult question. But in fact, they have not—they've answered an easier one: "Is it going to snow next week? Sure, it's cold enough today, it's been cold all week." Having grown up in Maine, I am familiar with this as a traditional way New Englanders speak to each other. Part of our culture is that we never answer the question asked. New Englanders pride themselves on never answering the question, instead applying attribute substitution and some deranged form of the Socratic method. It is a bit like playing poker with information. The person has the information, but until you ask the question the right way, all you will get is the attribute substitution, or deflection. Attribute substitution is substituting one question for another. I may ask you: How busy are you these days? Now you know how busy you are right now—so you're very likely to tell me how busy you are right now and think that you've answered the more general question of "how busy are you these days?"

We will always answer with information that is readily available. When we ask consumers which brands or products they have purchased in the past 30 days or the past two weeks, will they substitute? They sure will. I can remember what I had for dinner last night because I made it. I know what I will be having tonight because I was just told I am making it, but what I had any other night this week?—no top-of-mind idea. Our System 1 pathway is going take what information it has and provide the easiest answer that is tangential to the question or decision that will provide positive emotional payoff, even if it is as simple as the reward of answering the question itself.

Another and very similar heuristic is the availability heuristic, which is a mental shortcut that relies on immediate examples that come to a given person's mind when evaluating a specific topic, concept, method, or decision.

People are not aware of information that they do not have: we do not know what we do not know. We take whatever information we have, and our brain makes the best story possible out of that information; the information we do not have or do not know yet is not necessary. Our brain assembles the story, leapfrogging to conclusions without all the pieces.

For example, if I tell you about a technology brand and say that it is intelligent and innovative, you formulate an impression; you are thinking that it is a good brand. But the third word that I am about to say in describing the brand is "bankrupt." You do not wait for information that you do not have. You form an impression as I am providing the information based only on the information that you have.

In formulating impressions from incomplete information, we lean heavily on our emotional construct to fill in the gaps. Emotional information is prioritized over other information. How we feel is building the impression in the background and directs how we react. Using the same example of the technology brand, once I say "intelligent," you may feel impressed, interested, excited. I continue with "innovative," and the positive feelings may build. At this point, there is an emotional reaction to what I have said: you feel positivity. Then I drop "bankrupt" into the description and whoosh—emotions change and the impression changes. This all is happening in milliseconds. We are feeling our way to a conclusion with incomplete information, supplanting information with our emotional response.

Let us apply this to everyday decisions. We do not seek out a full information set; rarely is one ever presented. If we took in all of the options, contingencies and possible outcomes, we would be exactly like Dr. Damsio's patient Elliot, who was unable to make a decision. With only a rational construct, Elliot was impaired in achieving the goal of reaching a simple decision. The loss of the emotion structure was behind his decision-making failures. In our everyday decisions, unlike Elliot, we are receiving a constant stream of emotional feedback. The availability heuristic is pulling not only from examples that come to mind but also emotional outcomes.

One of my favorite cognitive biases, and one that is often misunderstood, is the anchoring bias. Anchoring describes the common human tendency to rely heavily on the first piece of information offered (the "anchor") when making decisions. This bias was the subject of many classes in law school on negotiation.

In the example of negotiation, the bias or belief is that we have an advantage if we go second. However, the advantage is to go first. Our brain tries to make sense out of whatever is put before it. We have an innate tendency to try to make sense of everything that we encounter, and that is the mechanism for anchoring. We cannot turn off our System 1 response to stimuli. The person who starts the negotiation establishes the terms, the range, and the emotional tone. The person who goes second cannot ignore that information; they react. It is impossible not to process the information and not be reactive. The reaction can be directed based upon where we want to end up in the negotiation, but the scope of the discussion has been shaped by the person who goes first.

When working with brands and messaging, understanding this cognitive bias is quite important. What is that first piece of information that consumers are going to anchor? I have frequently seen clients and agencies trying to squeeze in multiple messages or reasons to believe. Marketing creative and packaging becomes a treasure map that consumers must try to follow. There is disappointment when consumers do not understand or recognize the second-tier message, let alone the third. I have read many papers asserting that the human cognitive load is three things, but the fine print, the part most people ignore, is that if the first message does not land, then there is no hope for the rest, and the three-message theory is heavily reliant on repetition. That first piece of information is going to get the most cognitive weight. In the terms of my negotiation example, the consumer is always second. The initial offer is being made by the brand or product. The consumer is evaluating the information immediately through a System 1 process. It happens automatically, without cognitive control: taking in the visuals, the words, and the context; creating emotional feedback; and priming the behavioral response. This goes back to my earlier discussion about implicit responses being such a powerful predictor for behavior. The first impression formed immediately in our mind shapes how we perceive every piece of information that follows. The power of implicit information is that it provides insight into what our System 1 process has determined to be the important information for the behavioral response.

Another heuristic or cognitive bias is narrow framing. Narrow framing refers to the context in which a decision is made, or the context in which a decision is placed in order to influence that decision.

We tend to see decisions in isolation. We do not see the decision we are about to make in the context of similar decisions that we are going to make in the future. We are overly outcome-focused, and this occurs to the detriment of process. We view the situation narrowly, which is exactly the way in which the System 1 process excels and why a vast majority of our decisions occur within our System 1. I do not need to make a decision for tomorrow or to weigh how this decision will impact decisions and outcomes in the future. That requires a cognitive load for System 2. We default to making a decision for right now, with no regard to long term impact. Feel, then behave, and think about it later. Why? Because we are myopic—we have a narrow time horizon. To be more rational, we would have to look further in time, and we do not.

Green environmental choices provide a great example of narrow framing. Choosing a plastic water bottle or a plastic bag, letting the water run while brushing our teeth, and recycling are all decisions in isolation. The vast majority of people understand that we need to protect the environment in the long term. But as John Maynard Keynes said, "in the long term we are all dead"; we make decisions in the moment and figure out the details later.

Heuristics and Boots

Several of the heuristics discussed above can be applied to my ski boot purchase. While I was looking for a ski jacket for my son Drew, some emotional ember started to glow, sparking a want or need, which in turn created a motivation, and that emotional desire or goal then gathered into a single flame. I clicked on the boot section of the web site. My internal voice called to mind the scene from *Lord of the Rings* in which Bilbo Baggins is struggling with the power of the ring: "Why shouldn't I look for boots, I deserve them, I need them, yes indeed, need them." As images of boots started to fill the screen, an availability heuristic began to trigger, and immediate perfect examples of ski boots came to mind. My brain was now processing the visual information of the new boots, the false conclusion that my old boots were no longer functional, and an overwhelming emotional tug that created the false need for new boots. The cognitive bias then made the best story possible out of that information, and the information I did not have or did not know yet was not necessary. My brain had assembled the story, leapfrogging, without all the pieces of information, to the conclusion that, yes indeed, these boots were the boots for me. Go no further, it told me, I do not need more information, I can move directly to select and buy, and thus to emotional payoff. I was overwhelmed with feelings of success in accomplishing the goal, satisfaction, pride, and smugness that I had intelligently purchased not only boots but the right boots for me.

Or was it the cognitive bias of narrow framing? I clicked on the boots section under the influence of the same emotional drivers, but focused the decision with an immediacy context. The decision occurred in isolation from other contextual information. I was overly outcome-focused, and to the detriment of process. I did not account for the fact I was now going to have two pairs of boots. What was I going to do with the old boots? Even though the new boots were the same size, would they fit my skis? The bias had created a short timeframe for the decision, a false immediacy, and a sense that the decision, ignoring all other information, was binary. I could click "buy" and feel the surge of positive emotions or click away feeling remorse and disappointment. I was making the decision in isolation, with no regard for a longer time horizon or what impact this decision might have. Feeding that false immediacy was the impending holiday, the unknown of shipping, our annual post-holiday ski trip. Because I was myopic—with a narrow time horizon—I did not look further in time and consider whether this decision would have any impact on future decisions or events. If I stood back and rationally assessed the decision, there was no immediacy. I had planned to ski with my old boots right up to the moment that the new boots "need" popped into my head. The old boots were tried and true, satisfying all of the rational and emotional needs. With a rational mind I would have realized that the narrow framing of the decision was creating a new problem: what to do with the old boots. They were not throw-aways, and no one else in the family was the same size or needed boots. As I post-rationalized and began to build a case that I indeed had thought this decision through and could justifiably have two pairs of boots, it occurred to me that I now "needed" a new boot bag; after all, I am not uncivilized.

What about the anchoring bias? When I clicked on the boot section of the site, I filtered by men, my boot size, and my skiing ability, and because I am a cool dad I selected red and black to match my skis. The page loaded and boom!—there they were: the right color and size, a brand I recognized, last year's model, half price, and ready to ship. Granted, I asked for the information, but once the site returned the information in the form of these beautiful boots, it returned it in such a way that it created an anchor. The visual information became the first piece of information that I processed, in less than 13 milliseconds: 60,000 times faster than I processed the text and about 700 milliseconds before my conscious brain could recognize the stimuli as boots. The color, the shape, the physical and experiential contexts—all created emotional signals nourishing that flickering flame of emotional desire, saying "yes, this is going to fill that emotional void." The human tendency to rely heavily on the first piece of information offered (the "anchor") when making decisions was demonstrated in my response to the image. Once my brain recognized that what I was looking at were ski boots, I was already feeling satisfaction: positive emotions that these boots were the ones. I was then in a reactive state to a positive emotion. The first piece of information or anchor was the image, and all of the subsequent information was processed in the context of the first piece. I was like Renée Zellweger in *Jerry McGuire*: "You had me at hello." The next piece of information was the brand; Rossignol had all the right emotional equity. It brought back memories associated with the Rossignol rooster logo: race heritage, technology, quality, backcountry powder. It feels good to say Rossi's because that intangible bundle of attributes and emotions that is innately Rossignol eases off the tongue with a wry, intelligent wink. At this point I had processed only two pieces of information, all in a matter of milliseconds, and the cognitive anchoring bias continued to frame the next piece in the context of this cornucopia of positive emotion: the price—half price because they were last year's model. I had already clicked buy. There was no information that was going to disrupt the context in which I had already framed the decision. I was buying the boots, regardless of the price, and I would justify the cost. Hell, it had been over 20 years since I last bought boots; just think of all the money I had saved to put towards these beauties. They were almost free!

Chapter Six:
A Holistic View with Feel,
Behave, Think

Rear View Mirror

The cognitive bias that fuels our post-rationalized view of our decisions is hindsight bias. Hindsight bias is the inclination, after an event has occurred, to see the event as having been predictable, despite there having been little or no objective basis for predicting it. Let us talk about being wrong and being able to admit that one is wrong. John Kenneth Galbraith once famously said, "Faced with the choice between changing one's mind and proving that there is no need to do so, almost everyone gets busy on the proof."

We know that people try to make the best story possible, and in telling that best story we do not admit to or call out flaws or mistakes in our decisions. We tell the best story in a way that shows we did not make a mistake, and if something occurs that seems unanticipated, we in retrospect point out—and believe—that we did anticipate it. This is called hindsight. Once the events have unfolded, we fill in logical pieces to validate how we dealt with what just happened. It is not that we are all pathological liars; our brain is just making sense of what has happened and making a note that, should this happen again, it would be good to have this missing information. The main reason that we don't admit that we're wrong is that, whatever happens, we have a story; we can make a story, we can make sense of events, we think we understand them, and when we think we understand them we alter our image of what we thought earlier.

For a moment, let us bring this into the field of consumer insights. Consumers are not intentionally trying to mislead us; they just cannot explain the System 1 process that evoked their behavior. They cannot explain it because it was all subconscious, involuntary, fast, associative and emotion-led. They are forced to tell us in a very System 2 way how they arrived at the decision they made and why. Because the consumer is now looking at the decision with a hindsight bias, and they control the story they play back to us, it is very neatly rational—just like how I would tell you about why and how I bought those ski boots, and why I have used and bought Crest toothpaste for my entire life.

Consumer insights, marketing and brand managers have their own hindsight bias at play here. We ask for and take in the neat, rational consumer story and fit it into our own storytelling, which is also tidy and rational and fails to acknowledge the overwhelming role played by System 1 processes and emotion. We make sense of the consumer through the same single lens. What happened was anticipated, and how we explain it is by altering the story to fit the image of how consumers behave, believing that they think and then behave, and that the role of emotion is subservient to that of rational thought.

In the next section we will investigate the challenges presented when emotion is not considered as the driver of behavior. We will examine the disconnect created by focusing on what consumers think or how they behave without understanding how they feel. Here we will probe into my keyhole analogy: that without all three lenses, the conclusions or insights gained are flawed and lead to business decisions that miss the mark because we have a splintered view of the consumer.

The Say/Do Gap

I often speak about the Say/Do gap. It resonates well among audiences who are trying to understand consumer behavior. What consumers tell us about future behavior and what they actually do are disconnected. As consumers, we overstate intended behavior and fail to follow through. We see this universally in tracking data: metrics such as consideration and future purchase intent, which show intended future behavior that is never reflected in actual sales. Even in ad hoc work, consumers inflate how many products or services they will buy or use.

This gap between stated and actual behavior wreaks havoc in how we present and understand consumer data. There is a constant caveat that consumer attitudinal strength does not translate into behavior. In short, what consumers think is not fully reflected in how they behave.

As consumers, we are aspirational in our intent. We have wants and needs that are outside of our financial means or our current lifestyle. There are barriers that are not taken into account when a consumer speaks to future behavior. I have participated in many meetings with some of the most iconic brands discussing the disconnect between what consumers say and what they actually do. As a brand, how do you close that gap? Let me paint the typical scenario. On one side of the table is the marketing organization, and on the other side is the business or sales organization. In the middle is the consumer insights group. Marketing has been spending across various campaigns to support both the brand and the product. Attitudinally, consumers are in tune, and stated behavioral metrics show demand, but guess what? The sales organization is not seeing any change and the product is just trickling off the shelf.

Every year, eight out of ten new product launches, many of which have been tested, fail to meet their objectives or targets. What is missing? The consumer insights industry has been so focused on what consumers think and how attitudes can predict behavior that we have ignored how people feel and the dominant role emotions play in how we actually behave.

For a moment, reflect on behaviors you tell people you are going to do but do not follow through on: taking out a gym membership, organizing your closet, maybe meeting some friends you have not seen in a while. If I asked you whether you intended to go to the gym, you would say yes and sincerely mean it. Do you intend to go to the gym in the next week? Of course! You can probably tell me the name of your gym and the length of your membership and even provide an NPS or satisfaction rating. How long have you been carrying that gym card and not going? What is missing here is the emotional motivation loop. The emotion that creates the motivation to move you to the goal and the emotional payoff as you get closer to the goal are just not operating. The emotional drivers of the behavior are not aligned with the stated behavior. However, you can provide all types of feedback on your gym brand and experience, even though the last time you went was when you signed up a year ago. This example shows the disconnect between stated behavior and actual behavior when there is an emotional barrier. As a brand manager, knowing what those emotional barriers are, or how to overcome them or utilize them in marketing, would shrink the Say/Do gap.

Some organizations have gone as far as to ignore attitudinal consumer data and focus only on behavioral data. While they can see the clicks, purchases, and sales, they have no insight as to why they are occurring. In this extreme, organizations can see the types of people who are buying their products, profile who they are, and observe what they do, but they are left to draw conclusions in a very reactive way. It is like watching a chemistry experiment without understanding the interaction of the components. I can see that two items are mixed and the result, but with no knowledge as to why they reacted in the way they did. This of course leads to a great deal of modelling that can never account for the irrational consumer. The trigger for the behavior is never observed, only the outcome. A short reaction time is required when working within this framework. Can you react quickly enough to changing behavior even though you have no insight into what is driving it or when it will change? Not many businesses have the logistics in place to operate on a pure demand model. Of course, even if you can see the behavior and can nimbly shift, there is the problem of supply. With no product available, having a behavioral data view only lets you know what you missed. It may sound silly, but you cannot predict future human behavior based only on prior behavior.

An interesting example is the spike in demand for toilet paper during the Covid pandemic. Because toilet paper is bulky and takes up so much storage space, there is a very delicate balance in the treatment of it in the logistics system. Each retailer, based on past consumer behavior, orders and stocks only so much. This pure behavioral model goes up the chain to the producer. The margin of extra supply is very thin. Then our irrational consumer comes along. Yes, the pandemic was unforeseen, but what drove demand was squarely emotional. The toilet paper shortage of 2020 is going to be the topic of behavioral science papers for years to come. The consumer, faced with uncertainty, feels compelled to react: to protect and prepare. We don't want to feel uncertain, fearful, and not in control of what happens next. So why toilet paper? If people were rational, they would be thinking food, water, safety equipment, and medications. Well, ironically, the same quality that makes toilet paper a supply chain challenge—its bulky size—is what makes it emotionally valuable. People wanted to feel prepared, that they were doing something to protect their family. Putting a large item in an empty cart fills the cart. The bulky size created an emotional payoff of preparedness and satisfaction. In a time of panic, I want to feel safe and surround myself with things that visually show I am prepared. Toilet paper became the fastest way to add bulk to your supplies.

Everything that toilet paper represents is the antithesis of the apocalypse; it is soft, safe, and utilitarian, a symbol of civilization offering security in a time of need. No Sears catalog nailed to the outhouse door for me. I will survive this event with civilized dignity, and I will not be caught unprepared. So, we bought and hoarded toilet paper because it made us feel good. We felt that we were doing something to protect ourselves and our family. Toilet paper was an emotional security blanket, and what gave it that quality was in part its bulky size; it literally filled the emotional void with visual satisfaction.

No demand or behavioral model predicted that toilet paper was going to be the item we all needed. We all experienced what happens if an industry focuses on just behavior: we run out of toilet paper. Attitudinally, consumers post-rationalized around preparedness and not wanting to be left behind; toilet paper is a durable good with no shelf life, there was low risk if they over-purchased, and of course it is better to be safe than sorry. The "why" was missing. There was a gap between the behavior and what consumers were saying were the emotional drivers. Now panic buying is an extreme example, but the example does pointedly show that if we do not take emotion into account, the behavior itself leaves us in a very reactive position. How we understand and contextualize that behavior can be advantageous.

The Milk and the Bread

In New England we get snow in the winter, and sometimes we get quite a lot. For those of us who have been around for a while, the blizzard of 1978 is the measuring mark of all snowstorms. In the Maine town I grew up in, we were snowbound for three or four days and the National Guard had to come in with heavy equipment to clear the roads. The snowstorm had overwhelmed the state and local snow removal resources.

What is amazing about a New England snowstorm is the behavioral science experiment that plays out with every storm. It has fascinated me since I was old enough to walk to the corner store, and I benefited from the phenomenon in many ways while growing up in Maine. When a snowstorm or the dreaded Nor'easter is approaching New England, people begin to prepare. There is the rational preparedness instilled in every shrewd New Englander, like filling the gas tank of your car; prepping the snowblower, generator, and plow; and going to the town yard to get some salt and sand. Yet a behavior that occurs only in preparation for a snowstorm that is completely dominated by emotion is the rush to buy milk and bread. It does not matter how much milk and bread you have on hand, nor is it important that you could never consume all of this milk and bread before the storm has subsided. In fact, even in the blizzard of '78, no one in New England perished for lack of milk and bread. I am telling you this story to highlight another extreme example of emotion-based purchase behavior that is completely disconnected from rational thought and that, unlike the pandemic toilet paper example, occurs with some frequency every winter and has done so for a very long time. Knowledge of this emotional behavior can be capitalized upon if one understands the emotional drivers and the behaviors they trigger.

When a snowstorm approached, it was my duty, as the eldest child, to secure the milk and bread, not only for my family but for my grandmother. Off to the corner store I went, cash in hand, at a quick pace because time was of the essence. If you were too late, the milk and bread would be gone. People would be bustling on the street asking each other, "did you get the milk and the bread?" You may even hear that the local grocery store was running low because this storm could be bigger than '78! Now I always did my job and secured these essential supplies, but, in my mind, I always questioned why our survival was linked to milk and bread. The emotions at play are the same as those at work in the toilet paper example: the need to feel safe, secure, prepared. The purchases were a way to offset the uncertainty that the weather was bringing. Buying staples such as milk and bread provided emotional security and demonstrated that we were proactive and protective of the family.

When I was eighteen, I was driving refrigerated trucks for a local dairy in Portland, Maine. I now had control over the milk supply. I delivered to small mom and pop stores, like the one on the corner I used to go to as a kid, and to mid-sized supermarkets. While I had a regular driving route, we were commissioned salesmen. As soon as the first word of an approaching snowstorm hit the papers or airwaves, I knew that the emotion-based buying frenzy was coming. In fact, looking back, dairy drivers perpetuated it with carefully constructed small talk about the storm and what milk products were running low. This was our on-the-ground marketing campaign. As a salesman, I was also charged with ordering what was being loaded onto my truck, and when a storm was coming I would load it to capacity with milk. I had past behavioral data that I could rely on, but more importantly, I knew why the behavior was changing. I knew that the change was emotionally led and that it was going to end quickly. The balancing act was to meet the demand but not over-supply. Another wrinkle in the dairy business was that if the product did not sell and expired, drivers had to take it back, and it counted against their sales. Taking back too much expired milk would offset any gains.

The key was to understand the level of emotion that was driving the behavior. A small storm provoked less emotion; if a storm that was being called a Nor'easter was coming, there would be a lot of emotion. The days and hours building up to the storm required having conversations with customers and store owners and keeping up with the news because if the storm went out to sea or fizzled, you were stuck with a truckload of milk. At every touchpoint with customers, I was gauging the level of emotion about the storm. I would run a test case before I would put my big order in. In a small supermarket, before I completely unloaded the truck, I would fully stock the shelves and see how much sold during the time I was there. If the shelves were quickly almost empty, I knew I needed to load up. I had a few other tricks taught to me by the old timers to help immunize myself from loss if I ordered too much. As a kid putting himself through college, I was keenly aware of market dynamics, and, unbeknownst to me at the time, I was becoming a behavioral scientist. If I had not connected the behavior to the motivation or emotional driver, I would have missed an advantage. I also knew that the emotional driver and the strength of the emotions involved dramatically changed how people behaved. The behavior without the context would have only given me that the approach of a snowstorm equals a change in purchasing behavior.

I would not have been able to decipher the extent or real cause of that behavior without understanding the emotions of the customers and how those emotions contributed to the behavior based on the size of the storm. The holistic view of how consumers felt, behaved, and thought allowed me to take advantage of sudden shifts in all three focus areas and saved me from having a lot of spoiled milk.

Closing the Say/Do Gap

If we pay attention to just behavior, we lose insight into why the behavior is happening (e.g., the toilet paper shortage), and the ability to understand and impact change is lost. Focusing on just consumer behavior becomes a reactive test and learn environment that is not economically feasible. If we focus on just attitudes, we are stuck in consumers' post-rationalized narrative of why they did what they did or what they are likely to do from a System 2 perspective, as in the case of what I will tell you when you ask about my new ski boots. As we have already explored, capturing stated behavior disconnects consumers from how they actually behave, forcing them into a System 2 pathway of post-rationalization. The resulting disconnect is the Say/Do gap, where consumers attempt to explain a decision process that occurred subconsciously within their System 1 pathway. How can consumers explain what they will do when they don't even know why they did what they did in the past? We can only close the Say/Do gap by engaging consumers in the way they make decisions. The point of the snowstorm and milk story is to highlight that a holistic view of the consumer provides insight and advantage. If we explained the dynamic of increased milk purchase with snowfall, that would have produced a good insight or predictive model. But the amount of snow was not the real driver; sometimes it never snowed, and the storm went out to sea, but people still bought more milk. If we layer on attitudes about snow, then we get closer to the truth; people who remembered the blizzard of '78 had different attitudes, and those people who lived in rural areas were also attitudinally different from those who had access to a corner store. When we add in the emotions about the storm and the underlying motivations of safety, security, and preparedness, it becomes clear that, at this decision point, it was the emotion of the consumer that would drive the behavior. A holistic view was necessary because the behavior was never about the snow; the milk supply would not run out, and no one was going to perish due to a lack of dairy. Regardless of consumers' attitudes about dairy or the storm, it was the emotion surrounding the storm that drove behavior. These emotions were not based on facts, science, or rational, System 2 thinking. Even in 1978, no one died from starvation or was snowbound until spring. Looking at consumers through the decision pathway of feel, behave and think closes the Say/Do gap. Often it is the emotional "why" that is completely ignored, yet it is the origin of everything we are trying to capture and understand about the consumer. Ignoring emotion leaves us handicapped, constantly peering through the keyhole into the room. What we can see is limited and incomplete. This shapes our insight and ability to manage and react. It is only when we open the door, using the entire decision pathway, that we can have a complete view of the consumer.

A Brand is a Heuristic

When I start to discuss emotion, I often call upon David Ogilvy's statement "A brand is the intangible sum of emotions and product attributes." A brand is what a consumer feels and thinks of when they hear a brand name. It is everything a consumer believes about a brand offering—both emotional and rational. While a brand name exists objectively, what a brand is exists only in someone's heart and mind. As consumers, we buy brands, and a brand is a heuristic—a mental shortcut that we use to encapsulate that bundle of emotions and attributes. If we did not have brands, consumers would just be buying white boxes that said "food" or "product," with a list of contents. A brand, at its very core, is a System 1 device, and it enables consumers to make fast, associative, subconscious, emotional decisions with ease. Earlier I referenced work done at Cornell University that estimated we make 226.7 decisions each day about food alone and that the average adult is estimated to make about 35,000 decisions each day. We simply do not have the cognitive power to handle that amount of load. Brands take advantage of that by becoming a heuristic.

A brand is very much like a child. We can shape them, care for them, and provide direction, but once they are out in the world it is difficult to be there all the time. Perceptions, interactions, influences, and experiences that may be hearsay begin to shape the narrative of who and what this brand is. What are the emotions and attributes that will comprise that intangible bundle that is the heuristic of the brand? The job of marketing is to consistently tell and reinforce what the brand is and what it is not, shaping the narrative that goes out into the world so that consumers will adopt the narrative as their heuristic. Then, when the moment arrives, the consumer will leverage that shortcut to make a decision and choose the brand. Rational brand and product attributes are easily copied and hard to defend, while emotional connections are difficult to displace and replicate; they are unique, powerful and ownable. Brands quickly become interchangeable commodities when they compete on rational benefits alone.

In my work, I have consistently quantified the impact of emotion on behavior. The emotional pathway, much to the dismay of some marketers, is always a bigger and more impactful lever. The difficulty is that the emotional pathway is not a short-term play. It is far easier to message on a rational attribute—a new flavor, size, or price—and see the payoff in short term behavior. Unfortunately, many marketers and brands do not have the long term in mind when they need to deliver next quarter's sales numbers. We see the result of that in brand decay and a loss of emotional equity when the narrative from the brand is not creating affinity. Affinity is how close a consumer feels to a brand. What is that emotional connection? What emotional needs are being perceived and delivered by the brand, creating that subconscious motivational loop? It is not easy for consumers to explain their emotions, making it difficult to measure how or why they connect with brands through traditional attitudinal or System 2 methods.

To understand the role of a brand in consumers' lives, we need not only to acknowledge the role that emotions play and how they operate within our System 1 pathway, but also to employ tools that make the intangible tangible. Unfortunately, most people either ignore the role of emotion or acknowledge it and continue to hope that the inertia of the industry will save them. I have spoken to clients and colleagues who, sadly, have this strategy. What elephant?

The dominant role of emotion in purchasing decisions is demonstrated by one of the seminal brand stories of the 1980's: the Pepsi Challenge and Coca-Cola. In the early eighties, Coca-Cola was the dominant soft drink in the world, but Pepsi was slowly acquiring share. Coke was more widely available than Pepsi, but Pepsi was spending heavily on media campaigns. Pepsi began running TV commercials pitting Coke head-to-head against Pepsi in what was called the Pepsi Challenge. It went like this: a dedicated Coke drinker was asked to take a sip from two glasses, one marked Q and one marked M, and to reveal which they preferred. Much to the dismay of Coke, these challenges revealed that the Coke drinker preferred Pepsi. At first, Coke dismissed the challenges, then they replicated the results and began to get nervous. At the time, the thinking within the Coke organization was that maybe the American palate was changing, and the distinctive taste of Coke was losing its edge. Roy Stout was the head of Coke's consumer marketing research department at the time. He put forth to Coke's top management that the Pepsi challenge was about taste. In response, New Coke was born, and when tested in the same blind testing format of the Pepsi Challenge, it edged out Pepsi. The company's CEO, Roberto Goizuueta, called the new product "the surest move the company has ever made." Well, some of you know the ending of the story: a disaster ensued. Coke drinkers rose up in protest. I remember people buying and hoarding old Coke. My friend and I thought we would be rich selling our stash of old Coke. Stores were selling it at a premium, and t-shirts demanding the return of old Coke began popping up. It only took a few months for Coca Cola to release Classic Coke, the original formula, at which point New Coke disappeared into the marketing and business textbooks. The story of New Coke illustrates what happens when consumer insights rely solely on what people think.

In the Pepsi Challenge, most people prefer the taste of Pepsi in blind taste tests—that is, when they do not know which brand they are drinking. However, Coke to this day is still purchased more often by the majority of the cola drinkers in the real world. How do we reconcile this Say/Do gap? Consumers prefer the taste of Pepsi but buy Coke. Well, the rational thinking—the pitfall that Coke fell into—is that consumers will buy the beverage that tastes better. This has been deemed the Pepsi paradox. A team of neuroscientists led by Dr. Read Montague at the Brown Human Neuroimaging Lab at Baylor College of Medicine took the Pepsi Challenge to the lab to solve the paradox. The team repeated the experiment of the Pepsi Challenge but were collecting the System 1 response. Participants would drink the beverages while having their brains monitored with an fMRI, enabling neurologists to see what parts and functions of the brain were being activated. After being placed in the fMRI, participants were delivered the beverages in carefully designed straw-like tubes. In the first part of the experiment, the taste testing was blind or unbranded, exactly as the Pepsi Challenge had been constructed. In the second phase of the experiment, participants were exposed to an image of a can of Pepsi or Coke prior to receiving each drink to determine the effect of brand on preference and brand activity.

When the test was blind and participants were unaware of the brand, the preference levels and neurological responses mirrored the results of the original Pepsi Challenge. However, when participants were exposed to the brand, the stated preference was greater for Coke, and the brain scan imagery revealed significant differences in neurological activity validating that preference. There was synergy between how participants felt and their attitudinal response. When those tested expected Coke, there was significantly greater activation of the frontal area of the brain called the dorsal lateral prefrontal cortex, an area involved in decision making, memory and associations. Of even greater significance was the amount of activation within the amygdala and limbic system, which is the emotional center of the brain. What Dr. Montague was observing was the brands' "intangible bundle of emotions and attributes." Brand perceptions shape behavior. These perceptions are not reliant on direct experience and can be formed by cultural influences. The brand narrative is what lives in the mind of consumers, real or unreal, and the emotions the brand evokes are tied to that narrative. A brand creates an emotional expectation that if the consumer chooses it, the brand will deliver those emotions and do so consistently. Because the participants in Dr. Montague's experiment had been primed with an image of the brand, their System 1 construct created a goal or expectation around the experience of drinking Coke. When that goal was reached, Coke was delivered, and the synergy resulted in preference or behavior. Dr. Montague concluded that brand messages have insinuated themselves into our brain processes and lead to a behavioral effect, in this case preference.

Was the blind Pepsi Challenge marketing genius on the part of Pepsi? Intentionally removing the brand from the experience gave the sweeter Pepsi an edge. Did Coke follow blindly into a trap, after spending almost 100 years building an iconic brand? We do not buy products with blinders on, and the flaw of the Pepsi Challenge was putting consumers in a test that does not replicate how consumers buy and consume cola. By focusing on the rational response—do you like M or Q?—the challenge removed the emotional equity of Coke. Sadly, I see the Pepsi Challenge and New Coke story play out over and over again as people focus solely on rational System 2 drivers of behavior.

By ignoring emotion, we create our own Pepsi challenge trap. Consumers do not interact with unbranded products; their past or current behavior in isolation is not predictive of future behavior. What consumers tell us is often disconnected from what they actually do. The consumer is going to provide a nice, post-rationalized narrative without disclosing why they behaved the way that they did. As we have discussed, often consumers do not cognitively know why, as the emotional construct is operating behind the curtain within the realm of the System 1 pathway. So how do we understand and capture the impact of emotion on consumer decision making? In the next section, we will explore some of the passive System 1 tools that can reveal how consumers feel. We will examine how each method takes advantage of the System 1 pathway and provides us with a way to stop looking through the keyhole into the room and fully open the door to reveal the impetus to consumer behavior.

Chapter Seven: System 1 Tools that Capture Emotion

Visual Semiotics

What tools do we have to uncover and understand emotion? It would be fantastic if marketers were able to utilize fMRIs, MRIs, CT scans, biometrics, and other clinical neuro-measurement tools. However, those tools require expertise, they are expensive, and they demand physical participation. In the world of consumer insights, it is not feasible to have several hundred consumers undergo an fMRI every time we have a product or brand question. Measuring emotion requires a true passive System 1 tool. If we ask consumers what they feel, we know that cognitive bias and post-rationalization will provide the answer they think we want to hear. We also cannot dimensionalize the range of emotions a consumer may feel in a list. For example, the ancient Greeks had seven words for love. Having only seven words for love is a nice, neat continuum, but we know that other cultures have or had more or fewer words for love. The words available to describe emotions represent a limiting factor in understanding them. Psychologist Robert Plutchik created a model of human emotion which has been the basis of much of the work in the field. It begins with eight basic emotions and builds out to twenty-four, but it also creates secondary and tertiary relationships as well as opposites. We do not feel one emotion; we feel several emotions at a time that combine and interact. The absence of an emotion is just as impactful as its presence.

Semiotics is the study of sign processes, which are any activity, conduct, or process that involves signs, where a sign is defined as anything that communicates a meaning that is not the sign itself to the sign's interpreter. The meaning can be intentional and specific, or unintentional. Signs communicate through any of the senses; they can be visual, auditory, tactile, olfactory, or gustatory. Visual semiotics is a sub-domain of semiotics that analyzes the way visual images communicate. Visual semiotics can be utilized passively to understand the System 1 emotions conveyed and experienced by a consumer.

Humans have always used images to convey how we feel. A uniquely human trait is the ability to conjure up emotions about a particular place, time, or person at will. We not only recall those emotions, we actually feel them; we experience the emotions over again, which, as previously discussed, is core to memory creation. We surround ourselves with images that evoke emotions, such as art and pictures of our spouse, children, friends, pets, and vacations. All of that imagery we keep has a bundle of emotions associated with it. While we are not great at telling people how we feel verbally, we are very good at showing people how we feel with images. After all, our visual cortex has a direct line to our amygdala so that we can feel what we see. Our emotional construct controls how we visualize the world.

More than ninety percent of our brain operates on visual information, and other information is "visualized" to speed its integration. Our brain processes the 10,000 image-based impressions we experience every day through six semiotic structures: color, shape, physical context, social context, responsibility, and experiential context. Each of these structures contributes to our emotional response to what we are seeing. We have evolved to quickly formulate an emotional response to what we are observing; for example, is it safe or dangerous? This quick, emotional response to visual information provides the precursor and guidance to the behavior that follows. The structures are so powerful that we can take a static image and elicit the same emotions repeatedly and predictably. Since what we are taking in as visual information changes rapidly, our brain is constantly using the six structures to provide a constant stream of emotional feedback. Our System 1, pattern-seeking construct is subconsciously assessing any visual data so that we are feeling what we see, and we behave in accordance with that emotional feedback. While the decomposition of what we are seeing into the six structures happens simultaneously in milliseconds, for ease of explanation I will discuss them in an order of magnitude and in the context of a static image.

- **Color:** The colors of what we are seeing provide the core base emotions. The primary color of an image is felt first and is the most powerful. The colors we see provide the core emotional influences, and they dominate all others in our visual and emotional interpretation of the world. For example, red is energy, both positive and negative. When we see something red, our emotional construct provides attention. Red flowers are attractive, red dart frogs are deadly, and both immediately enact an energy-based emotion. We quickly see a color, formulate an emotion, and are biologically primed to behave or react.

- **Shapes**: The primary shapes in an image provide psychological context. They are the modifiers of the primary emotions. For example, round things protect or are safe, and sharp angles require caution. The shape of what we are seeing in an image provides degrees to the primary emotion: how safe or how much caution in the context of the primary emotion.

- **Physical Context:** Physical context is our role or place in the image: are we close or far away, involved or passive? What do we expect that we will physically experience, being a part of the visual we are seeing? For example, in the case of an image of a party, is our role to help, to attend and enjoy, or is the party for us? How we perceive our physical context is heavily influenced by culture and is the second largest set of influences on how we feel when looking at an image.

- **Social Context:** The social context is our social role in the image: where we see ourselves fitting into what is going on in the image. Our social context is defined by the primary dimensions of our social life and roles: are we included, excluded, dominant or submissive? For example, if the image is of people dancing at a club, would we be dancing, observing, waiting to leave, or not even there?

- **Responsibility:** Responsibility is the who or what is responsible for the primary change in the context of the image. For example, if the image is of a crying child with arms outstretched towards the viewer, it evokes an emotion of responsibility—or not. Would you pick up the child or look around for someone else? If there is action to be taken, who, in your mind, is responsible for the action? It could be you or a product or something else: culture, nature, or a natural force.

- **Experiential context:** The experiential context is comprised of secondary emotions reflecting individual experience/individual emotional conclusions. I feel the primary emotion and that in turn evokes another layer of emotional evaluation. For example, I see red rose petals scattered as a pathway in my house. I feel visual energy from the red color as an emotion of seduction; knowing they are from my wife, as context, also evokes the emotion of happiness. Context evaluation, starting with color plus emotional change, leads to new emotional evaluation. Emotional understanding is the understanding of the emotional transaction or transition.

I often explain how our brain automatically decomposes images into these structures by using the example of looking at a piece of impressionist art, such as a painting of water lilies by Monet. If we stand back, we see the complete image, and while the image is simply a composition of paint structures, our brain fills in the pattern and the water lilies look complete. As we move closer to the painting, the image starts to decompose; we see some of the layers and textures and realize that the painting is not "complete," but rather shapes and colors on top of each other. When we are very close to the painting, the image further decomposes to the point that we see the brush strokes, the thickness of the paint, and that the painting is not two dimensional. The image as a whole is lost, and we focus on the components. As our brain processes an image it is taking these structures and feeding that information into our emotional construct to immediately process how we feel about the stimuli. The image evokes a multidimensional set of emotions that we then can then react to or behave in concert with.

Using visual semiotics to understand consumer emotions involves decoding the emotions tied to the six structures. The essence of art is that every person can view it and have a different emotional connection. Every image carries different emotional elements or codes, some positive and some negative, but if we ask a consumer to create a set of images that convey how they feel, we can then start to quantify their emotions using the same elements that evoke the emotions in our brain.

The use of visual semiotics to understand and convey emotions has its roots in clinical psychology. The use of visual semiotics to understand underlying emotions involves having patients create a collage of images that, taken together as a whole, represents how they feel. By then aggregating the set of images and analyzing the emotional codes and structures of the images, the clinician can understand with a passive technique the emotions being conveyed and their intensity.

The patient is not using their System 2 pathway because the structures and emotional codes are not conscious. We cannot override the visual/emotional connection. In the terms of my Monet example, my System 2 brain sees water lilies, while System 1 feels the emotions conveyed by the image.

I am fortunate enough to work with a brilliant visual semiotician, Michael Sack, who co-developed a set of images with a clinical psychologist who worked to understand and improve communications among non-verbal autistic children. This imagery set has its roots in construct psychology, which discovered that elements of images (colors, shapes, and other qualities such as size relationships, distances, etc.) conveyed specific emotional qualities; for example, red conveys emotional energy and blue conveys calm. Sack went on to validate the existence of 144 emotional codes derived from the six visual semiotic structures and the relationship of those codes with specific emotions. A mathematical approach was used to identify the relationships between the codes, emotions, and structures. It is this mathematical relationship that is behind the U.S. patent Sack obtained in 1992.

This patent is the very first intellectual or business model patent ever issued to the market research industry. In the industry, all patents before and most since this date are machine patents that describe unique data collection or data presentation methods, not analysis techniques. The validation of the relationship between the meanings and the symbols was done by two professors of astrophysics at Princeton University. Why astrophysics, you may ask? Because the relationship model uses the same mathematics that proves the existence of black holes. Emotions, and their impact, are an intangible, like gravitational forces. Emotions exist and impact everything around us, but they are hard to measure, and while they are always present, we rarely acknowledge the role that they play. The unseen forces of gravity shape the world and universe around us. Nothing is more powerful; even light bends a knee. The impact of our emotions is similarly pervasive; emotions are an ever-present force influencing all that we perceive and how we respond. Michael Sack created a system to code verified symbols to identify non-random associations and apply the emotional meaning of these associations using an approach which has proven itself in the market for over 30 years.

Feeling what we see is an evolutionary advantage. We can see and feel safety or danger. We begin our lives associating shapes, colors, and structures into simple codes of good and bad. Round big things that you cannot swallow are good, long pointy things are bad. A red-hot stove is bad, but blue, cold water is good. I am oversimplifying a bit, but we reinforce what visual structures "mean" emotionally when we teach our children about the world around them. From the earliest cave painting to the latest digital art, every visual is an emotional expression, and we react to each one subconsciously. We cannot override this response, and we are limited by language and biases in how we explain it. This is why a passive System 1 tool using visual semiotics is so powerful. We have a universal visual language that we can tap into. We all speak it and understand it. We have evolved with it and, unbeknownst to our cognitive self, we rely on it every day.

The challenge is that we need to decode images passively because the process is System 1; once we ask a consumer how they feel about an image, the post-rational System 2 brain kicks in, along with our biases and language limitations. There are a lot of image-based emotional measurement tools that are not passive System 1 tools because they rely on the participant to associate an emotion with an image. These tools fail to take into account the basic fact that we feel multiple emotions at the same time. The choice of the emotion associated with an image by the consumer is restricted to a list of emotions provided. Returning to my example of the Greeks and how they defined love with only seven words, it was conveniently narrow but not realistic. How the emotional list is defined shapes how the System 2 brain will choose to tell the story. Hindsight bias and being the narrator of our own story comes into play. We will tell the emotional story we want to convey to put us in the best light. The word of caution here is that not all image-based emotional measurement systems are measuring passive System 1 emotions.

Eyes of the World

We experience the world through imagery, and all information required for both System 1 and System 2 decision making comes to the mind in the form of images. If you look out the window at a green, budding spring landscape, or listen to the Jerry Garcia tune playing in the background, or run your fingers over the smooth plastic surface of a keyboard, or read these words line after line down the page, you are perceiving, and thereby forming images of various sensory modalities. The images formed are called perceptual images. But you may stop looking at the landscape, or listening to Jerry, or touching the keyboard, or reading the text, and distract yourself. Maybe you are thinking about a cup of coffee or about whether it is going to rain today; maybe you are still thinking about what I said about images. Any of those thoughts is constituted by images, regardless of whether it is made up of shapes, colors, movements, tones, or spoken or unspoken words. Those images, which occur as you conjure up things in the past, are known as recalled images.

By using recalled images, you can bring back a particular type of past image, one formed when you were planning something that has not happened yet, but that you anticipate will happen; for example, washing your car this weekend. As the planning process unfolds, you are forming images of objects and movements and consolidating a memory of that fiction—the future washing of the car—in your mind. These are images of something that has not happened yet and may never happen, but they are the same as if it had already happened. These various perceptual images—recalled from the real past or recalled from plans for the future—are constructions of your brain. All you know is that they are real to you and that other people make similar images that are comparable. We share our image-based concept of the world with other humans, and there is remarkable consistency in the way different individuals construct the essential aspects of the environment around them (color, shape, space, texture, sound).

In their book *Genius in the Shadows: A Biography of Leo Szilard, the Man Behind the Bomb*, William Lanouette and Bela Silard write, "It is often said that thought is made of much more than just images, that it is made also of words and nonimage abstract symbols. But what that statement misses, is the fact that both words and arbitrary symbols are based on topographically organized representations that can become images. Most of the words we use in our inner speech, before speaking or writing a sentence, exist as auditory or visual images in our consciousness. If they did not become images, however fleeting, they would not be anything that we could know."

The point is that images are the main content of our thought, regardless of the sensory modality in which they are generated and regardless of whether they are about a thing or a process involving things, or about words or other symbols in a language which corresponds to a thing or process. Hidden behind those images are the essential components for all of our thinking. We are dependent on our brain's fast, associative, emotional, pattern-seeking System 1 process to connect and make sense of these images.

Implicit Testing

I briefly spoke about the Implicit Association Test (IAT) and its application with cognitive biases. In its simplest application, implicit testing gives us insight into which of the two distinct paths of decision making is involved in a decision: System 1, the implicit fast path, or System 2, the explicit slow path. The measurement of reaction time in conjunction with fMRI scans of the brain which visualize the brain processes has demonstrated that emotions operate within the System 1 path. Implicit testing is very good at identifying not only that cognitive biases exist, but that those biases are comprised of emotional elements. The stronger the emotion, the quicker the reaction time. I do not have to "think" about the response—I feel the response. We often speak about people's passion for topics or activities. The more passionate they are, the more engaged and reactive they can be when challenged or prompted. Politics is a good example of a subject about which people tend to implicitly respond. While implicit testing helps identify the degree of unconscious attitudes and feelings, it does not tell us how people are feeling or what their attitudes are. Another way to think about it is that a cognitive bias or heuristic is a combination of emotion and beliefs. Those beliefs are based on rational facts or truths to some degree, and, in this combination, the higher the emotional factor, the more implicit the response. Using implicit testing, we can understand if the decision is System 1 or not. We can also understand, based on the degree of implicitness, if the bundle of emotions and attitudes is more heavily weighted in emotion.

Implicit testing comes in many forms, and there are different tactics to be employed depending on what the user is trying to capture and understand. IAT places a consumer in binary choice setting in which the stimuli are associated either positively or negatively with the topic or brand presented. For example, I am presented with brand A and asked to agree or disagree on the attribute "trustworthy." Because the test is timed and binary, it provides three pieces of information. The first is whether I agree that brand A is trustworthy. The second piece of information is determined by looking at my response time. How many milliseconds did it take for me to make that association? Was it fast and implicit or slow and explicit? Did I have to employ cognition using my System 2 pathway, or did I associate "trustworthy" with the brand so quickly that my cognitive processes physically could not have directed the behavior of association? The third piece of information is the degree of implicit or explicit response. Did I really have to think hard using my System 2 pathway to arrive at the answer— a long explicit response in milliseconds—or was my response very quick? The more implicit and rapid, the greater the emotional weight. The degree of implicitness is a very important component that is often not optimized in an analysis.

Over what amount of time in milliseconds do subconscious System 1 processes occur? Well, that is one of the biggest areas of debate in the clinical and behavioral science fields. As technology has progressed and fMRIs have become readily available, the range has become not smaller but rather larger because we are finding that stimuli are processed at different rates. In 2014, as part of an MIT study, it was measured that visual stimuli were being processed by the brain in as little as 14 milliseconds. Combing through the scientific literature, we can arrive at a generalized range. As in the case of a room full of economists, there will never be agreement, but I will put forth the following as guiding principles. The moment that a stimulus occurs (e.g., time = 0ms), the brain automatically starts to process it. It takes somewhere between 100 – 200ms for humans to detect a stimulus and respond to it. At this point, the brain has not had sufficient time to necessarily recognize what the stimulus is; it has simply recognized that there is one. By 400ms the brain is able to discriminate stimuli, again without requiring conscious processing, and 150-300ms later, we can effect a response, demonstrating that the stimulus has been correctly identified. Importantly, all of this occurs before the stimulus has been processed by conscious brain mechanisms, and therefore any response obtained after 200ms but before 800ms is considered uncontaminated by conscious thought processes. I have seen the upper range posited to be as high as 1,500ms.

There are a lot of factors that come into play, such as the complexity and composition of the stimuli, how the stimuli are presented, and who is evaluating the stimuli. We do not all read or process information at the same speed. In work that I have conducted, I consistently see that age is a factor in response time. Older people are a little slower on the uptake, especially once they cross the threshold of sixty. A good implicit test is going to be designed taking these factors into consideration to minimize their potential impact. Another unique view is looking at the degree of implicitness associated with stimuli in isolation. Often approaches look across stimuli and create relativity calculations (comparing the speed of stimuli response to each other to determine implicitness). While this method may seem appropriate, a consumer will never evaluate the stimuli comparatively. The stimuli are either implicit or not, and while relativity is nice to know, it does not change the System 1 response the consumer is having.

Another area that is debated is the composition of the stimuli. Images are processed much faster, and we respond implicitly to them more quickly; our response to text is much slower, and the response to a combination of images and text varies widely. There is a belief that "complex" stimuli such as longer phrases cannot be processed implicitly, but the science just does not support that belief. Here is a simple example. If I show you "Solve $E = mc2$," do you implicitly think "this is Einstein's theory of relativity" or "energy equals mass times the speed of light squared"?; maybe you see the picture of Einstein with his tongue out, or you are reminded how much you hated algebra. Your brain does not switch over to System 2 and start solving the equation. We do not read all the words in a text, we do not pay attention to all the nuances in an image, and we certainly do not take in all of the components of a product. Our System 1 pathway takes in just enough information to associate it quickly to a pattern, evoke an emotion, and suggest a behavior. No matter how complex we think the stimuli are, our brain is never going to consider all the pieces; there will always be some degree of implicit response.

Complexity comes into play in what consumers are asked to associate the stimuli with and whether or not it fits with their System 1 response; if it does not fit, then it is handed over to System 2 and the response then becomes explicit. If complexity of stimuli dictated what can be processed by implicit System 1 response, we would have a hard time navigating the world. Our System 1 pathway exists because of the complexity of stimuli!

An IAT can take many forms; if the answer choices are not binary, an Implicit Response Test (IRT) would be employed. An example of an IRT would be if I were presented with the attribute "trustworthy," but my answer choices were Brands A, B, C, and D. I can only allocate trustworthiness to one brand. While I may consider all of the brands to be trustworthy to some degree, this method forces discrimination in that I must choose only one, and the test is capturing the time it takes to make that choice. I will implicitly and quickly choose the brand I have the most affinity to. Again, the stronger the emotional composition, the more implicit the response. If I struggle to choose (employing more rational think time), then the response is explicit, and the tester can see that there is less of an emotional connection. IRTs can be built into many traditional question types as the capture of the time data in milliseconds is the only necessary component. Implicit testing often requires an additional behavioral science technique. Some of those techniques are disruptors and some are primers.

A disruptor is an exercise that requires System 2 cognitive thinking, disrupting what would be an associative, fast, subconscious, System 1 task. A good example is the Stroop test, named after John Ridley Stroop, who identified the effect and published his observations in 1935. In psychology, the Stroop effect is the delay in reaction time between equal and unequal stimuli. The effect has been used to create a psychological test that is widely used in clinical practice and investigation. The effect can be demonstrated by presenting subjects with a mismatch between the name of a color and the color it is printed in (e.g., the word "red" printed in blue ink instead of red ink). When asked to name the color of the word, individuals take longer and are more prone to errors when the color of the ink does not match the name of the color. Using a Stroop test or disrupter is a way of re-setting or calibrating a behavioral process. Using it in combination with an implicit test, we can force consumers into a disrupted state to calibrate the implicit measurement. Without actually seeing the brain activity on an fMRI, we can trigger the two systems and observe them at work through reaction time.

Priming is a phenomenon whereby exposure to one stimulus influences a response to a subsequent stimulus, without conscious guidance or intention. For example, the word "surgery" is recognized more quickly following the word "hospital" than following the word "pizza." Priming can be perceptual, associative, repetitive, positive, negative, affective, semantic, or conceptual. While there is debate around the duration of priming effects, their onset can be almost instantaneous. Priming works most effectively when the two stimuli are in the same manner of experience. For example, visual priming works best with visual cues and verbal priming works best with verbal cues.

Priming is used in conjunction with implicit tests to understand biases and the strength of those biases. The long-standing Harvard implicit response test on race uses priming. The priming mechanisms set the brain to associate A with B, and the implicit test measures the inconsistencies between the primed association and what a person implicitly associates. The outcome here is to separate what we portray as outwardly true (how we project with our System 2 pathway that is in control of the narrative) from what we inwardly or emotionally feel (through our implicit System 1, which is hardwired as actually true).

We all have a complex set of biases, such as what we would categorize as simple preferences—like choosing coffee over tea. We have preferences among both things we have experienced and things we have not experienced. Food is a good example. I could go through a grocery store and very easily tell you the foods I would not eat, even though I have never tried some of them. We also have social biases: things we do not say in public, but we cannot help but think. Implicit testing is a wonderful tool to discover implicit beliefs and truths that a consumer would not readily put forward. What consumers do not tell us can be our greatest strength or liability, but that information is not going to come through in the post-rational, System 2-filtered version that is traditionally captured in consumer insights.

Projective Questioning and Shared Experiences

While people are very willing to volunteer information explaining their actions, those explanations, particularly when it comes to the kinds of spontaneous attitudes and decisions that arise out of the unconscious, are not accurate, and in fact sometimes they are plucked out of thin air. When marketers ask consumers to provide feedback, how much trust should we be placing in those answers? Is the most accurate way to find out how consumers feel about something to ask them directly? How we ask the question will impact how people respond and what we learn or believe we have learned.

Projective techniques originated in the field of psychology and are similar to Rorschach ink blots and Thematic Apperception tests. Qualitative researchers have long adapted these approaches for use in consumer research. Projective questions or exercises are designed to uncover people's deeper feelings on a topic and are purposely set up to ask key questions in an indirect way. These techniques are used to obtain a deep understanding of emotional needs, barriers, and motivators. Projective techniques remove any bias and pressure on the consumer to provide an acceptable answer since they are explaining how "other people" feel, behave, and think. We are more open and forthcoming with our responses when we describe what "other" people have said or done because we can visually see the reaction of the person asking the question and either separate ourselves from the "others" if the reaction is negative or include ourselves if the reaction is positive.

We are very good at observing what others do, and we often emulate or want to emulate that behavior. This is the basis of all social influencer construct marketing. Projective questioning techniques allow us to ask consumers about observed behaviors while removing themselves "personally" from the response. We innately mimic and tend to behave like our social peers. We are profoundly social creatures, and our biology has driven us to the adaptation of social environments as an evolutionary advantage. The human brain has not just been shaped by its interaction with the physical environment but has evolved most importantly to adapt to the social environment in which we live. As neuropsychiatrist Louann Brizendine states, "Our brains have been shaped by hundreds of thousands of years living in status-conscious hierarchical groups."

We are so in tune with others around us that we have the ability to project ourselves into the minds, feelings, and actions of others. Let's revisit mimicry in the context of emotion-based behavior. In the early 1990s, neurophysiologist Giacomo Rizzolatti and his team at the University of Parma were investigating the motor system of the brain—the part of the central nervous system involved in movement—when they discovered, quite by accident, what Dr. Rizzolatti named mirror neurons.

To better understand the human brain, Dr. Rizzolatti was studying the electrical activity of the motor neurons of a macaque monkey. Using hair-width electrodes, the researchers were investigating the activity of the premotor cortex, the part of the brain involved in planning and initiation of movement: the thought before a physical behavior. As expected, the motor neurons would fire or activate when the monkey performed a physical action, such as moving an arm to grab an object. One hot summer day, the team left for lunch and accidently left the equipment on and the monkey hooked up. When they returned, one of the graduate students working with Dr. Rizzolatti was eating an ice cream cone. The monkey watched the student lick the cone with attentive focus. To the surprise of the scientist, each time the student licked the ice cream, the electrodes signaled a spike in activity of the motor neurons of the monkey, despite the fact that the monkey remained motionless. Instead of physically carrying out the action of licking the ice cream cone, the monkey was imitating the same activity in its own mind, firing the same motor neurons as it imagined eating the ice cream cone.

Dr. Rizzolatti had serendipitously uncovered that empathy—putting yourself in someone else's position—is mediated by neurons in the brain's motor system. These mirror neurons give humans the capacity for shared experiences by enabling us to project ourselves into the minds, feelings, and actions of others. Dr. Rizzolatti explained, "We are exquisitely social creatures. Our survival depends on understanding the actions, intentions, and emotions of others. Mirror neurons allow us to grasp the minds of others not through conceptual reasoning but rather through direct simulation. By feeling, not thinking."

The concept might be simple, but its implications are far-reaching. Over the past decade, more research has suggested that mirror neurons might help explain not only empathy, but also autism and even the evolution of language. "Take all these lines of evidence together, and it seems clear that mirror neurons are one key to understanding "how human beings survive and thrive in a complex social world," says neuroscientist Vittorio Gallese, one of Rizzolatti's colleagues at the University of Parma. "This neural mechanism is involuntary and automatic," he says. With it, we do not have to think about what other people are doing or feeling: we simply know. "It seems we're wired to see other people as similar to us, rather than different," Gallese says. "At the root, as humans we identify the person we're facing as someone like ourselves."

Projective techniques lean heavily on our ability to observe behavior and our desire to emulate others and mirror empathic emotions and behavior. We can project how others feel and behave quite readily because we subconsciously experience it ourselves. A simple example of a projective form of questioning is asking, "Which flavor of ice cream do people like the most?" I am not asking what flavor you like, but rather what others like. There is immediately anonymity in the response. The response is not you; it is them. This removes the pressure on the response. If you say "chocolate" and I respond back, "really? I like vanilla," it becomes quite easy for you to agree that you also like vanilla, but for some reason other people like chocolate. The response biases are diminished. When people respond to such questions, they are pulling from their observations of others—their friends, family, colleagues—and their experiences or behaviors of the collective. If I directly ask you, "How did that movie make you feel?", again, the response puts you in a vulnerable state, and more likely than not the response will be very directed, looking for my reaction before any further discussion occurs. However, if I ask you how others felt about the movie, because you are removed from the response, you can expound upon the great deal of laughter in the theater and still hold back from disclosing that you may or may not have found the movie funny. Projective techniques also allow people to project their true thoughts and beliefs onto other people or even objects. The person's real feelings can be inferred from what they say about others. These are all examples of a third person projective technique. Another technique is to disconnect the person's experience from the topic completely, so they are playing back stronger observations. For example, if I ask you if you drink coffee and you say no, and then I proceed to question you further on coffee consumption behaviors, you are forced to draw more deeply on your observations of others. Unless the topic is very esoteric, we probably have a long list of observed behaviors that we have never engaged in but are pretty knowledgeable about. The point here is that indirect questioning about experiences, emotions, and behaviors that we observe is able to provide an accurate picture of both a collective and ourselves. We are biologically equipped to play back and emulate how others feel, behave, and think.

For the Love of Toothpaste

My affinity for Crest toothpaste and its evolution from childhood brand to a continuing preference demonstrates the power of brand as a heuristic and cognitive bias and presents a good example of why implicit truths and barriers need to be accounted for. Keeping with my David Ogilvy definition of brand as an "intangible bundle of attributes and emotions," when I see or hear the word Crest there is an immediate conjuring of positive emotion and a mix of generalized efficacy attributes. The brand Crest is my mental shortcut for toothpaste. In my mind, the toothpaste category is defined by how I feel about Crest and what I think to be true about Crest and competitive brands. When I am in the store and toothpaste is on the list—a goal—I am on subconscious autopilot when I am in the toothpaste section. I am looking for the brand and for the visual cues that are associated with Crest. I am scanning the aisle for the big red C with blue REST. The brand offering and packaging have evolved and, not surprisingly, the red, white, and blue color combination has been adopted by the entire category. It has become harder to just look and immediately see Crest despite the big red C. Once I see that big red C, my brand heuristic fires off in milliseconds. The emotions inspired by my childhood experience in the crowded bathroom, my own kids' toothbrushing experience, my confrontation with my wife when she tried to introduce me to another brand, my French-Canadian dentist's scary warnings about cavities, forced fluoride rinses in grade school, the unpleasant smell of drilled teeth when I had four cavities, my mother's terse response when I asked for blue AIM toothpaste: all culminate at once.

Accompanying that crescendo of emotion are the faint words of some 1970's advertisement, my mother's rationale that 9 out 10 dentists agree and recommend Crest to fight tooth decay and cavities, Dr. Contois telling me to brush my teeth with a fluoride toothpaste like Crest, and the fact that I have not had a cavity in forty years, proving that mom was right. The brand has done what it says it will do: clean my teeth and prevent tooth decay. The emotional side of the equation is satisfied, and what I believe to be the rational truths are also satisfied, so in that fraction of a second my brain reinforces the brand connection to those elements and instructs me to put the toothpaste in the cart. There is no need for the System 2 thought process to intervene—no need to break this behavior or decision down into advantages and disadvantages. Buying toothpaste is as subconscious for me as walking up a flight of stairs.

Now the people in charge of the Crest brand at P&G would be elated to read this brand story, and I must admit I did commit a faux pas one time in using this example with a competitive toothpaste client in the room. However, the discussion turned to how to discover and use this information. Starting with implicit truths, if I were provided a list of claims, attributes, or "reasons to believe" and asked to associate them with a brand, not surprisingly, based on the above, I would associate them with Crest. If we took that same list and put them in an implicit response test, we would be able to see the implicit strength of each and where I may have had to dedicate more "think time" or engage in more explicit thought. The attributes with the highest implicit responses are my implicit truths: rational claims that I believe to be true even though I may have no information to support or contradict them. These implicit truths are behavioral economic advantages for Crest and barriers for other brands. It is very difficult to displace implicit truths without a long and sustained marketing campaign. However, if we looked at the attributes that provoked more explicit thought, these are the behavioral economic advantages for competitive brands.

Now from the story I have told, you may have deduced that in the 1970's it was all about tooth decay and cavities. As knowledge about oral health has advanced, the focus has come to include gum disease. I do not think I was given a packet of floss by a dentist until I was in my mid-twenties. Of course, fashion has changed as well, and it has become desirable to have teeth so white it is sometimes cartoonish. If my implicit association test included a list of claims on gum health and whiteness, the processing of those claims would be more explicit. My brand heuristic for Crest does not include gum health and whiteness directly; they would be tangential to the brand. These two areas would be ripe for competitive brands to gain an advantage. The weaker implicit responses would also be a warning to Crest that the brand is not addressing those rational messages, despite the strong emotional connection demonstrated by customers like me. Absent any implicit testing to gain insight into this System 1-driven behavior, both Crest and competitive toothpaste brands would be disadvantaged. Crest would not see its Achilles heel, and competitors would be mindlessly trying to displace a cognitive bias that has strong emotional roots. Both Crest and competitors would benefit from knowing that part of my brand heuristic is the package design and the visuals that I have associated with the brand. When I am at the shelf, I am not looking for the brand; my visual brain is fast-seeing for the structures, primarily color and shape, that immediately signal Crest.

This is where visual semiotics would come into play. If I were to engage in a visual semiotics exercise, it would be clear that I have a strong emotional connection to Crest, and that the emotions are multifaceted. My emotional connection to the brand has little to do with what the product does and everything to do with how the product makes me feel. We would also see that I define the category ideal through the lens of Crest. The emotions I feel about the ideal toothpaste would be aligned with how I feel about Crest, and other brands would not evoke the same emotional response even though I have never experienced those brands.

My reaction in this situation provides a good example of hindsight, or post-rational bias: the other brands are inferior because I do not choose them. As the narrator of the story, I will paint my decision in the light most favorable to me making an intelligent decision. For Crest, knowing the emotions that connect me to the brand creates an opportunity for the brand to message to me in a way that reinforces the emotions that I already feel and connect with the brand. I am more open to the message when it reinforces those pre-existing emotional connections. If P&G were to look at my behavioral data—my past purchases—they would see I tend to buy the old school Crest cavity protection line. I am open to the messages of gum health and whitening if they are coming to me in a way that aligns with my emotions about Crest.

On the competitive side of this example, knowing how I emotionally connect to Crest and that I emotionally define the ideal and category through the lens of Crest provides the emotional talk track of how a competitor must message to me. The competitor now knows that gum health and whitening are areas of opportunity; I do not have strong implicit associations with Crest in those two areas. The competitor also has insight into the qualities of the emotional wrapper in which they need to deliver those messages. Lastly, they would know that cavity protection and fluoride are my strongest implicit associations to Crest, the rational attributes that I will tell you are the reasons why I buy the brand.

You may never shop for toothpaste the same way. Because most of our behavior is System 1-driven, it really takes an effort to deconstruct a process as simple as buying toothpaste. However, in 2020, P&G sold 283 million units of toothpaste, which translated into 1.074 billion dollars in U.S. sales. Total sales of U.S. toothpaste amounted to about 3.11 billion USD in that period. Fortune Business Insights states that the global market size was 17.75 billion USD in 2019 and is projected to reach 21.99 billion USD by 2027.

I reference those sales and market numbers because often people, whether they are in charge of a brand or insights, believe that the System 1 process does not apply to them—that somehow their brand or category is exempt from human evolutionary behavior. The use of fast-moving consumer packaged goods (FMCPG) as an example is often looked down upon because of the price point and how FMCPGs are marketed and sold. If insight into human behavior can drive the 18-billion-dollar global toothpaste category, imagine what it can do for the "special categories." If a human is buying your brand, product, or service, then yes, the System 1 pathway is involved. We cannot shut it off, no more than we can stop our heart or breathing upon command with our mind. We can ignore it, and many brands and insights groups do, but it is still there.

My favorite tall tale is that certain categories are more rational and complex because the behavior is less frequent, like the durable goods or financial services categories. The bigger the decision, the more emotionally charged it is! It would only take a glance at the news headlines to see emotion-based behavior in action. Cars are a good example; if we made rational decisions, why do sports cars exist?

Why are we not all driving the modern-day people's car or electric vehicles? Pure rational thought would lead us to a utilitarian product. Luckily, car brands are ahead of the game when it comes to emotion. They know that people have a relationship with their cars and that, as with any relationship, emotion is the key. Just because the decision seems complex or consumers do research and comparisons and tell you all the facts and features they considered does not negate the overwhelming role of emotion.

Motivational Pathways Through Laddering

Clinical psychologists first introduced the laddering technique in the 1960s as a method of understanding people's core values and beliefs. The technique is powerful because it provides a simple and systematic way of establishing an individual's core set of constructs with respect to how they view the world. Laddering is well established in the field of psychology, and its success has led researchers in a number of industries to adapt its core tenets to their fields. Laddering is typically used to encourage self-analysis of behavior and motivations. Applying this process helps us to gather a more complete list of "consequences" and climb towards the hard-to-reach "values." Early marketing practitioners conceived and refined a model for describing the linkages between customers' values and their overall purchasing behavior.

According to the Means End Chain theory, there is a hierarchy of consumer perceptions and product knowledge that ranges from attributes (A) to consumption consequences (C) to personal values (V), as follows:

Attributes—At the top level of this hierarchy, attributes are most recognizable by individuals. Individuals recognize the attributes of a product or system easily. For example, I like this car because it is a sports car and it is fast.
Consequences—In turn, the attributes have consequences for the individual. For example, the sports car makes me feel young and attractive. Each attribute may have one or more consequences for any given individual.
Core Values—Finally, each consequence is linked to a core value of the person's life. For example, the sense of youth makes me feel free.

This is the traditional view, and if you pick up any book or article on Means End Chain theory you will see that the A-C-V sequence forms a chain, or ladder, that indicates the relationship between a product attribute and a core value. Now let us really dissect this theory through the lens of the System 1 and 2 pathways and the role of emotion. The attribute is the rational component that our hindsight bias will play back as the reason why we chose the product. The attribute is also part of the brand heuristic: what we believe the brand will rationally deliver. If I put the brand Porsche in front of you, the attributes that come to mind may be fast, sports car, expensive, racing, red, and so forth. We like to believe that consumers buy rational attributes, features, and functions—that they buy a product for a utilitarian purpose. We see consumers in our mind with lists and spreadsheets, checking and cross-checking all the attributes and features until they reach the logical decision. For some people and some decisions, this "research" is indeed done to arrive at a final consideration set. However, while all this rational crosschecking is being done, we are guiding the decision, influenced by our emotions, to arrive at—lo and behold!—the smart decision we subconsciously already arrived at.

Ponder for a moment the last "researched" decision you made. What brands did you start with? What brands did you discard? And after all of the research, did you buy a brand or product completely different than where you started in your consideration set? We quite literally research our way into the decision we want to make; we just want that gratification of conducting research and establishing a set of attributes to justify why we did what we did.

The attribute at the top of the hierarchy is a rational feature; in my example, the sports car is fast. The need, want, and desire is speed. The "why" is what leads us to the consequence, and this is the emotional motivation; here is the System 1 influence at work. The consequence is the underpinning emotion that is driving us to the goal. A fast car delivers emotions associated with youth and attractiveness. We want the fast car to feel the positive emotions. What is driving that emotional connection? The core value of feeling free, or freedom. Our core values are emotional constructs that are also within our System 1 pathway. Core values are emotional tenets that create the goal and begin the motivation process, which is driven by the consequence. The emotions of the consequence are providing feedback, positive or negative depending on how far we are from the goal. Once the goal is reached, the consequence emotion is satiated.

Means End Chain theory suggests that personal values play the most dominant role in directing individuals' choices. These personal values are individuals' core beliefs and are relatively stable perspectives that have an overwhelming emotional impact. Drawing on Milton Rokeach's groundbreaking work in Terminal Values, and the refinements introduced by David Forbes' research on Human Motivation, I will posit that there are nine core values:

1. Security (To feel safe, confident, and free from worry)
2. Empowerment (To feel equal to the task, capable, and free to act)
3. Belonging (To feel connected through relationships to other people in my world)
4. Identity (To do things that reflect how I see myself and my personal taste, style, and values)
5. Engagement (To do all the activities of my life in a way that feels great—exciting, productive, absorbing)
6. Nurturing (To do things with others that make me feel good—loving, liking, caring, and cooperating)
7. Mastery (To feel full actualization of my personal talents and strengths)
8. Achievement (To have good results from my life's activities, and outcomes of which I can feel proud)
9. Esteem (To have a standing in my social network that makes me feel respect and admiration)

We can collect all the A-C-V ladders for a given domain to form a Hierarchical Value Map that illustrates all the major means-end and attribute-consequence-value connections and describes individuals' behavior based on their core values. Typically, these maps contain many product attributes that are linked to a smaller set of consequences, which are, in turn, mapped to a core set of individual values. While particular individuals are likely to have specific nuances to their sets of ladders and value maps, we can recognize and document high-level patterns across different customer types or personas. The real power of the Means End Chain model is that it uncovers the emotional pathway that leads to an important set of functional attributes or properties. While some people show and discuss the ladders beginning with the rational feature because that is how we like to believe we operate, to align it with our biological and behavioral systems, we would evaluate the hierarchy from core motivation down to the rational feature. The attribute is not driving the behavior; it is what we point to when we are asked why we behaved the way we did. We feel, behave, and lastly think.

Laddering and creating motivational pathways help us understand not only the emotions that drive the behavior, but those evoked by each attribute. From a messaging and packaging standpoint, this provides a roadmap to create the emotional wrapper that consumers want to feel while engaging with the product or brand. Each rational attribute fulfills an emotional need, and it is the emotional payoff that creates the behavior. We buy what makes us feel good, and the door prize is delivering the functionality we want. To some this may sound like a Gordian Knot, but the challenge is discerning where the beginning and the end of the rope are. Do we design for the emotional need or the rational function to complete a task—what some marketers would call jobs to be done? If we only look through the System 2 lens of rational and functional attributes, we have a splintered view; we are ignoring that jobs to be done require motivation to do them, and jobs that provide positive emotional feedback become important, and those with negative emotional feedback become disregarded or abandoned. A complete and holistic view will always provide a better answer.

In the next section we will examine how behavior can be changed and influenced through emotion: how what a consumer feels not only controls their decision and behavior but also contributes to the rational narrative they create, even when it is false or inconsistent with the rational information. Here we discuss how irrational the consumer really is and how marketing can win or lose the hearts of consumers. What consumers buy are emotions they can easily associate with the brand or product. We will discover that what consumers emotionally perceive and associate is more powerful than any rational benefit in driving behavior.

Chapter Eight: Changing Behavior Through Emotion

Sensation Transference

Dr. Louis Cheskin was a scientific researcher, clinical psychologist, and important marketing innovator. He observed that people's perceptions of products and services were directly related to aesthetic design and named this relationship sensation transference. Dr. Cheskin spent most of his life investigating how design elements impacted people's perceptions of value, appeal, and relevance. He demonstrated that, on an unconscious level, people do not make a distinction between the package and the product. The product is the package and product combined. He also discovered that most people could not resist transferring their emotions or feelings about the packaging to the product itself. In the 1930s, he founded the Color Research Institute of America in Chicago, which was later renamed Louis Cheskin Associates. He was one of the first marketers to use customer-centric methods and to value direct customer input above marketers' expectations or guesses about customers' needs.

In 1951, Dr. Cheskin published a groundbreaking book, *Color for Profit*, which initiated a scientific approach to color and design. His work focused on three core concepts:

1. Good taste has little to do with how well a package design sells.
2. Asking customers what they think of a package design is not a useful way to measure effectiveness. Surveys and polls do not

measure unconscious reactions; what consumers do, not what they say, is what matters.

3. Colors have symbolic subconscious meanings that impact our behavior.

If you just had a moment where you said to yourself, wait, 70 years ago Dr. Cheskin was already writing about unconscious System 1 influence on behavior, the Say/Do gap, and visual semiotics? Yes, and that shows the level of inertia within marketing and consumer insights. As the famous quote often attributed to Albert Einstein goes, "The definition of insanity is doing the same thing over and over again and expecting a different result." Yet here we are in the asylum going about our merry way. Cheskin said,

"Psychoanalytical findings concerning the nature of the unconscious show how naive we have been in basing marketing research on the assumption that human beings always are able and willing to reveal their true feelings, or to predict their own behavior. From psychoanalysis we learn that only a small proportion of the individual's total experiences (or emotional life) is within his conscious grasp. Some of an individual's experiences can be recalled by a casual association and some by special techniques, but a good part remains forever beyond the reach of the conscious mind. We generally recognize that we forget much of our past. But difficult to accept is the knowledge that these presumably forgotten experiences are really not forgotten but remain in the unconscious where they continue to exert tremendous power over our behavior. Conscious feelings and intentions, therefore, are often overwhelmed by forces hidden deep in the unconscious. It is the unconscious purpose rather than the intellectual reasoning processes that generally determines how an individual will behave. If marketing research, then, is to predict reliably what people will do, it must have procedures and techniques for discovering unconscious motives, purposes and needs."

Most people make unconscious assessments of a product, service, or event based not only on the item itself, but on subconscious sensory input associated with the item, which all contributes to one general impression—whether intended or not, or accurate or not. Our implicit or subconscious associations are influenced by what we see, what we believe, what we feel, and our biases. This is what Dr. Cheskin pursued as sensation transference. We do not have to experience the product, and what we believe does not have to be true, but rather our beliefs must only be perceived and associated in a positive manner. Visual semiotics played a large role in the products and brands guided by Dr. Cheskin. He evaluated and influenced the colors and shapes of packaging, as well as the physical, social, and experiential contexts of the products' use. The impressions the packaging creates in customers' minds are transferred directly to rational concepts of value, price, quality, affinity, and emotion. These, in turn, create and fulfill emotional expectations of satisfaction whilst leaving rational breadcrumbs that consumers can point to as the reason why they bought the product.

Adding to this concept of sensation transference, the heuristic of brand—"the intangible bundle of emotions and attributes"—showcases that part of that bundle is what the consumer expects the brand to deliver. This expectation is shaped by the brand advertising and positioning and how the brand is presented: not just the packaging, but who is using the brand, what it is being used for, and where it is being used. The story we shape around the product becomes innately part of the product. When a brand strays from that perception, we begin to question our heuristic.

Dr. Cheskin's storied career impacted iconic brands and products such as Marlborough cigarettes, Betty Crocker, Duncan Hines, the Gerber baby, McDonald's, and Disney, to name a few. Though Dr. Cheskin's process was created and perfected in the 1950s and 1960s, it is just as relevant to marketing today as back then—more so, perhaps, with the rise in experiential branding and marketing. Indeed, marketing tests continue to confirm the validity of Dr. Cheskin's sensation transference phenomenon.

The Taste of Color

In 2011, Coca-Cola found out quickly that people can taste color. To raise money for polar bears, Coca-Cola began selling its flagship Coke in white cans that featured polar bears. This was the first time that Coca-Cola came in anything but a red can. Now, to be sure, polar bears have been a symbol Coca-Cola has used for many years during the holiday season and at other times as well. However, the white cans were rejected because customers believed that the Coke sold in the white cans tasted different. The representatives of the company (with the "New Coke" fiasco in the back of their minds) stated in no uncertain terms that they had not changed the recipe. So how could this change in taste perception occur?

One of Dr. Cheskin's pioneering projects was in the category of margarine. Margarine, when first produced, had a white color that consumers found unattractive. Dr. Cheskin was able to show through testing that people liked margarine and butter equally when an artificial yellow coloring was added to margarine to replicate the look of butter. He also added a foil wrapper, to associate the product with high quality, and put a crown on the package to create Imperial Margarine. Even more related to Coke's issue—and something that should have made them more cautious in changing the color of their can—was an experiment Dr. Cheskin did with 7-Up. He added 15% more yellow to the color of the can. The result? People thought the recipe had changed and now contained more lemon!

Coca Cola's white holiday Coke can was dead two months before the campaign was scheduled to end. If, for the first time in 125 years, you plan to offer Coke in containers that do not feature red, you had better be sure your customers are open to such a disruptive change to their brand heuristic. This story shows how reliant we are on our subconscious perceptions and how they can impact something we believe is rational, like taste.

Dr. Charles Spence is an experimental psychologist at the University of Oxford. He is the head of the Crossmodal Research group, which specializes in research about the integration of information across different sensory modalities. He is the modern-day Dr. Louis Cheskin. One of his most referenced studies demonstrated that potato chips that made a louder, higher-pitched crunch were perceived to be a full fifteen percent fresher than softer-sounding chips. The experiment showed that food could be made to be thought to taste different through the addition or subtraction of sound alone. Spence published his results in the *Journal of Sensory Studies* in 2004. The paper, written with a post-doc colleague, Massimiliano Zampini, was titled "The Role of Auditory Cues in Modulating the Perceived Crispness and Staleness of Potato Chips." Before the sonic-chip breakthrough, Spence had worked almost exclusively on how an understanding of the neuroscience of audio and visual stimuli could help in designing better warning signals for drivers.

In his office, Dr. Spence maintains a rogues' gallery of failed products—he had no part in their creation—and he gleefully demonstrates their sensory miscues. Sitting atop a filing cabinet is a special-edition white-colored can of Coke. For Dr. Spence, the can is evidence of the power of a package's color to alter the perception of the taste of the contents. His lab has repeatedly shown that red, the usual color of a Coke can, is associated with sweetness; in one experiment, participants perceived salty popcorn as tasting sweet when it was served in a red bowl.

Our System 1 pathway can create an experience so real that it is real! We can observe a package and, with no interaction with the product, formulate a set of expectations. Those expectations can change how we feel, what we perceive, and what rational descriptors we will attach to that product. What we implicitly believe drives our behavior and provides the illusion of rational decisions, when in fact we are confirming what our System 1 has already narrated. This is cognitive confirmation bias. When the pattern does not fit, as in the case of Coke in a white can, we not only expect a difference—we can experience a difference. No amount of post-rational thinking is going to convince us otherwise. As Coke found out, there is no winning against implicit perceptions.

More Cheap Wine Please

An interesting study on wine conducted by researchers at the Stanford Graduate School of Business and the California Institute of Technology went beyond our ability to project our feelings onto packages and products, discovering that emotions can be invoked simply by price. When we consume a more expensive product, we not only anticipate a more positive emotion, we feel it, and that emotional encoding impacts how we will behave in the future.

The subjects were told that they would be trying five different Cabernet Sauvignons, identified by price, to study the effect of sampling time on flavor. In fact, only three wines were used—two were given twice. The first wine was identified by its real bottle price of $5 and by a fake $45 price tag. The second wine was marked with its actual $90 price and by a fictitious $10 tag. The third wine, which was used to distract the participants, was marked with its correct $35 price. The subjects' brains were monitored using an fMRI.

Not only did the subjects consistently believe the higher-priced wine tasted better, but the fMRI brain scans also revealed that there was greater activation in the pleasure center of the brain when the subjects believed they were drinking the more expensive wine, even though the wines were identical. Price was changing people's emotional experiences with a product and, therefore, the outcomes from consuming the product.

Previous studies have shown that it is possible to change people's reports of how good an experience is by changing their beliefs about the experience. For example, moviegoers will report liking a movie more when they hear beforehand that it is very good. The wine study went beyond these previous studies to show that the neural encoding of the quality of an experience is actually changed by a variable such as price, which most people believe is correlated with experienced pleasantness. The brain encodes pleasure because it is useful for learning which activities to repeat and which ones to avoid, and decision making requires measures of the quality of an experience. We have a general belief that cheaper products are of lower quality, and this translates into specific expectations about specific products. Once these expectations are activated, they translate into emotional self-fulfilling prophecies that impact our behavior. What becomes clear from similar pricing studies is that people have no conscious realization that price is actually influencing their behavior. The non-conscious effect of price alone impacts how we feel about brands and products before we ever choose or consider them.

For the Love of Cars

I could not discuss how we transfer emotions to products and how we can be subconsciously influenced by the package itself without discussing cars. Dr. Cheskin helped market and develop one of America's most iconic cars, and one of Ford's most successful: the Ford Mustang. He also influenced the Lincoln Continental, the country's first modern "luxury" car.

We can all remember our first car, whether it was a family hand-me-down, a gift from Grandma, or that junker that someone had for sale down the street. Our first car often symbolizes a life stage, and it is such an emotionally important acquisition that the make and model of one's first car is a common online security question for account and password retrieval. It is right there in the drop-down menu with the street you grew up on, your favorite book, your favorite teacher, where you are born, and of course your mother's maiden name. My first car was a 1977 Pontiac Grand Safari station wagon, in a dark green with faux wood trim on the sides. The interior was also a horrible shade of green, with fancy, wood-looking plastic accents. It was an eight-cylinder beast that guzzled gas and was about as cool as I was as a teenager—not that I am any less nerdy now. It was the family car, and I had access to it as long as my mother did not need it. I was responsible for putting my own gas into it, and given its fuel economy of maybe 10 miles per gallon and its propensity to break down, I would never put more than $5 of gas in it at any given time because I did not want to have expensive gas stuck in the tank when the beast refused to move. What I loved about this car was that it was so big that I could accommodate my entire entourage of friends, and their friends, and still have room. The car was the longest (slightly more than 19 feet) and heaviest (5,300 pounds) that Pontiac ever made. My car was always the car we took places because I could take everyone and everything we needed. I had a lot of adventures and misadventures in that titanic car.

Cars have personalities; we give them names, we assign a gender to them, we talk to them, and we care for them for a long time. A car is a product that becomes part of your family; it is a statement of who you are and who you may want to be, and it encapsulates where you are in your life stages. I have owned twelve cars to date, not including my boys' three cars. Each car is a story of who I was at the time when I owned it and who I am now. My wife and I recently bought a new family car, and she cried when we were emptying the old one to trade it in. She said, "we have a lot of memories in this car of our boys and family, and I am having a hard time letting it go." We reminisced about some of those moments: the first dent, the tear in the console, the stickers on the back, the mystery damage that none of our son's would admit to. Every piece of wear and tear had a story. For ten years, vacations, trips, school pickups, practices, and learning to drive were all part of our experience with this car. We took our last picture with our car, with mixed emotions, and we let it go. I must admit, just writing this is raising tears and memories; what strange irony, as I am experiencing the very topic of discussion.

Whether we are car people or not, we all have implicit associations about car brands. The "intangible bundle of emotions and attributes" that our mind can conjure up is very strong, even though we may never have experienced the brand. In fact, car brands conjure up such distinct emotions, attributes, and personalities that they are often used in qualitative work to understand other product categories. If I asked you to define yourself as a car brand, it probably would not take long for you to respond. Sure, you may not reveal publicly that you see yourself as Jeep—capable of overcoming obstacles, rugged, dependable. It may be more posh to say Range Rover: still a brand with a rugged explorer heritage, but more worldly, and more associated with luxury and refinement.

As Dr. Cheskin successfully proved, people cannot resist transferring their emotions or feelings to products themselves. Our brand heuristic is strong in the car category because we spend a lot of time with our cars. How we feel and how we want to feel are inextricably entangled in the product and its features. What motivates us to choose a brand or model of car is directly a result of those emotions. Because the purchase of a car is a pricey and long-term commitment, we believe we are very rational in how we approach the task, and we have the spreadsheets to prove it!

We start with a list of wants and needs: seating capacity, number of cup holders, cargo space, and so forth. We also have a short list of brands in mind that we have an affinity for either through experience or based on what we implicitly believe to be true. In my case, we owned a Honda Pilot; it had three rows of seating, all-wheel drive, and all the amenities that one might look for in an SUV that was going to haul three boys, their friends, and cargo. It was the first Honda I had ever owned. My bias, based on my experience, was in favor of Japanese cars because of their reliability and longevity. Somewhere in the back of my mind was my dad warning me never to buy an American car if I expected to keep it for a long time. Along with that faint voice was the experience as a kid at a car dealership of my dad asking for the day and month a car rolled off the line. When I asked why, he told me never to buy a car that was built on a Monday because after a weekend of beer drinking the mechanics on the line were not at their best; he called them blue

Monday cars. Naturally, as a man of contradictions, my father has owned only American cars his whole life, with the exception of one in 1984, and he was a mechanic for the Navy.

If, at the early stage of decision making in purchasing a new car, I was subject to an implicit response test, it would become very clear that, at a brand level, I had a strong implicit affinity for Japanese cars. It would also be discovered that German cars, while not delivering on the same attributes or emotions, were also brands that may be in the consideration set, but for different applications. The implicit subconscious advantage was given to Japanese brands. My System 1 pathway could easily associate in a fast and involuntary way, triggering my underlying emotional motivations, which in turn would provide positive emotional feedback that reinforced choosing a Japanese brand. I would feel good about that decision, and I could rationally back it up with some of the attributes I have already mentioned. My basic gut instinct would be fulfilled. A good choice, a safe choice, a reliable choice: it is a family car and I want to feel safety, reliability, and protection, not worry or concern. On the other hand, I am the appointed driver when the family needs to go somewhere, especially the long-haul trips. While I do enjoy driving, a few driver perks or luxuries were in my mind as well. With these considerations in mind a set of brands was developed, and models were identified that delivered on the primary rational attribute: capacity. I did not start out looking for capacity, the rational functional component; I began with how I felt about brands and the heuristics they provided.

At this point in the decision journey, if I were to undergo a visual semiotics exercise, I could clearly show you, using images, how each brand and model made me feel and what my ideal emotional set would be. We would be able to see where each brand and model delivered and under-delivered against the ideal set of emotions that were driving my short list. Going even further and applying Mean End Chain theory or motivational pathway laddering, we could take each rational feature and function that I said was important to me and understand the bundle of emotions and the core life values that were driving the want and need of those functions and features. I was not buying the car based on what it did—drive the family to and from destinations—but rather in the service of the very same emotions that made my wife cry when we said goodbye to our Honda, and the same emotions that haunt my memories about other cars I have owned.

The core life value in my case was security. When you are on a family trip, everyone you love is right there: your whole world in a tin box. You will do anything to protect your family. The decision of which car to buy is driven by that emotional motivation to keep the family safe. What emotions would you want to feel if safety was the goal? Maybe a sense of reliability, a lack of worry and concern, confidence, certainty. These are the emotions and traits that I implicitly believe that Japanese brands deliver. For example, we live in New England, where it snows, and I would tell you I need all-wheel drive or four-wheel drive. Having four-wheel drive in the snow makes me feel in control and confident. Those emotions of control and confidence in turn ladder up to the core value of feeling secure.

While there is a list of product features that I would tell you are needed in the car, those rational product features needed to deliver first and foremost on the underlying emotions. To further complicate things, they must be delivered within my brand heuristic and compatible with my biases. I was not looking for just four-wheel drive; it was four-wheel drive among a set of brands that, as the Japanese organizational expert Marie Kondo would say, sparked joy. A Chevy Suburban has amazing capacity, it is four-wheel drive, and it is used internationally to protect heads of state, but Chevy as a brand does not fit with my heuristic. What I implicitly believe about Chevy—that intangible bundle of attributes and emotions—keeps it from the consideration set.

Just like every consumer in the digital age, I amassed data and created lists. These were the rational features and benefits that I would cite in the narrative explaining why I bought the car I bought. I went so far as to place our Honda side by side with other cars we were looking at so we could compare the room and capacity visually. I had the numbers— the cubic feet of space for each part of each car—but as my wife so elegantly said, she wanted to feel how much room there was. In the end, the feeling of space trumped all the math.

If the purchase of a car, a complex and expensive purchase, were rational, I would be open to all brands, and if I followed the principles of economics, I would choose the lowest-priced product that delivered the features I needed—not wanted or desired, but needed. My purchase decision would be utilitarian in nature: four wheels that delivered me from point A to point B. As I hope you can see from my example, emotion was the prevailing force in my decision-making, setting a pre-determined course that I was destined to follow. If asked about my purchase, I would create a rational narrative to justify why I chose the car that I did, telling you about the features that I never considered, such as the six driver modes, the full touch screen control, all of the extra safety features. I would tell you about the great price and how I haggled strategically. However, now you know that none of that is the true reason I bought the car I did. I was guided by my emotional construct to choose a car that satisfied my emotional needs, and I justified and explained that subconscious process with rational elements because buying a car is, after all, a rational decision!

Getting It Right

Subaru is a brand that understands and leverages emotion and how people feel about cars. I owned a Subaru, and there is not enough room in this book to tell all of its stories. Subaru advertisements are focused on love. The company understands that we emotionally bond to our cars, that life happens in your car. The ads' tagline is "Love: it's what makes a Subaru a Subaru." In one ad, called "Making Memories," a father is cleaning his Subaru before he gives it to his daughter, and every item he finds in the car causes him to flash back to one of his daughter's life moments. The sequences portray happy and sad memories, as the daughter grows up before his eyes. At the end of the ad the father lets go of the car and his daughter as she drives away, but the memories are always there. A car is a time capsule of memories, and Subaru does a fantastic job in capturing that emotional connection between the brand, the product, and how we feel.

In another TV spot, called "Father Daughter," the brand uses the same creative device of memory and emotion, but shows a father speaking to very young girl in the front seat about being safe: having the mirrors and seats properly adjusted, staying off the highway. He hands the keys over to the young child, who then becomes a grown-up teenager. The ad uses the emotion of worry and concern for safety through the creative device that we always will see our children as kids that need protecting. We cannot always be there, but we can put them in a safe car. The brand again is tapping into the core life value of safety. The product is not the hero of the ad; it is the emotion we feel as parents, giving up control as our kids get older. We want them to be safe and protected.

Yet another ad, called "For All Your Love," shows the memories of a family through an old dog that walks through items that symbolize life stages, and as the dog walks through each set of items it becomes younger, until it is a puppy jumping into the back of the car. Here the brand is using two emotional devices: our memories connected to our cars and how we feel about dogs. The car and the dog are both providing love to the family. There is not a rational message anywhere: not a feature or a price, not even a model call-out. Why? Because Subaru knows that how we feel is going to drive behavior and that core values supported by emotion are most powerful at creating a brand heuristic. As in my own car-buying example, how we feel about a brand determines whether the brand even makes the cut.

In the final section, we will widen our view once again to the pathway to human decision making and the overwhelming role of emotion. Consumers are not making well thought out, rational decisions. All the rational claims and reasons to believe are for naught if they are not connected to the emotions that are driving the behavior. We will break down the decision process in the context of the System 1 pathway and the influence of the emotional construct. And finally, with an understanding that we feel, then behave, and lastly think, I offer a call to action to apply this framework to achieve a holistic understanding of consumer decision making. Attempting to understand the consumer without acknowledging the decisive role of emotion will always leave us with an incomplete view and never answer the question of why consumers behave the way that they do.

Chapter Nine:
Feel, Behave, Think

Decisions, Reasoning, and Emotion

The terms "reasoning" and "deciding" are often used interchangeably, and while their meanings are interwoven, reasoning is the process through which we come to a decision. The word reasoning implies that there is some logical strategy for producing valid inferences that requires support structures of attention and memory, but its meaning includes not a wisp of emotion or feelings and how these impact our assessment of the innumerable options that are generated for selection.

A pure System 1 decision example is the case of a baseball traveling fast toward you. There are options for actions: move out of the way, catch the ball, or let it hit you. Each response has a different consequence. However, if you have never caught a baseball, that option may not be viable. Depending on how fast the ball is traveling, catching it with your hand may not be possible. You may miss catching the ball. You could move out of the way and reduce the consequences of not catching the ball, or do nothing and be hit. To select a response, we use neither conscious knowledge nor conscious reasoning strategy. The requisite knowledge was once conscious when we first experienced that fast-moving objects which strike us may hurt and that avoiding them is positive. Our brains solidly pair fast objects that could strike the body with danger, and the automated subconscious response is to avoid danger, driven by the emotion of fear. You cannot willfully override your System 1 response to avoid being struck. Sure, you can stand there and take one to the noggin, but your brain is telling you to duck, protect yourself, pain is coming, and that response will happen regardless. Your emotional construct is clearly presenting two options: safety, which feels good, and danger, which feels bad. We will always seek the positive emotion. In this example, the motivation is simple—avoid pain—and the goal is also clear: avoid the ball so there is no pain. The payoff is that avoiding the ball results in no pain and safety.

A more complex example is choosing a career. To arrive at a decision, we rely on the supposedly clear process of deriving logical consequences from assumed premises and making reliable inferences which, absent any emotion, allow us to choose the best possible option, leading us to the best possible outcome. But what is different from the first example? Choosing a career has more parts to it, the response options are more numerous, the consequences have more ramifications, and those consequences are often different immediately and in the future, thus posing a conflict between possible advantages and disadvantages over a longer time frame. The complexity and uncertainty are so large and overwhelming that reliable predictions are just not easy to come by. On top of this, the great number of possible options that could be presented if this were a rational process would require processing a great many facts and hypothetical actions and matching them against goals of varying time lengths and ultimate goals. All of this would require a systematic and proven method. Based on the very obvious differences between the two examples, it is not surprising that people assume that they involve entirely unrelated processes or mechanisms. However, despite the differences in the level of complexity of the two scenarios, we have but one neurobiological core. While our System 2 pathway may play a bigger role as the decisions become more complex, our System 1 pathway and emotional influences are omnipresent.

As we saw with Dr. Damasio's Elliot and Phineas Gage, damage to the part of the brain that is responsible for emotions is accompanied by an inability to make decisions, even those as simple as choosing what to eat for lunch. The lack of an emotional construct impairs the ability to determine the consequences of a potential decision or its gravity; is it important, such as a choice about a financial investment, or trivial, such as whether or not to have a turkey sandwich? We further explored this with Dr. Klin's autistic patient Peter, who demonstrated the inability to make good decisions without emotional feedback.

What is a good decision? A good decision is one that is advantageous. A lot depends on the frame of reference of the goal that was set. A good decision must take into account such things as personal and social outcomes: the impact of the decision on survival, shelter, health, employment, finances, social standing, and so forth. Deciding well also means deciding in a time frame that is appropriate for the gravity of the decision or choice at hand. The best decision may not be an available choice.

Let us walk through an abstract situation which calls for a decision. The brain reacts to the situation by rapidly creating scenarios of possible options and related outcomes. In our consciousness, these "what if" scenarios play out as imagery as our pattern-seeking System 1 pathway compiles and attempts to connect a vast set of unstructured data. The process does not occur in the context of a tabula rasa, but rather it is replete with a diverse repertoire of imagery that has been generated to tune into the situation we are now facing. This imagery enters and exits our consciousness in such a manner that we cannot encompass it fully; it is a literal flood of scenarios, options, and outcomes.

If we were completely rational and solely reliant on our System 2 pathway, we would be like Dr. Damasio's Elliot and Phineas Gage. We would take the different scenarios apart and apply an econometric cost/benefit analysis to each of them, all the while keeping in mind the subjective utility of each, and determine which would maximize that utility (good) and which would lessen that utility (bad). We would consider the consequences of each option at different points in the projected future and weigh them as losses or gains impacting the overall utility. Of course, most problems do not have binary alternatives, and the scenarios for decisions will begin to compound exponentially. The options and outcomes could be infinite. Now if this was how we made all decisions—pure rationality—it clearly would not work. At best, a decision may take an inordinate amount of time, longer than acceptable if action or behavior is needed with any immediacy. We may not even end up with a decision, so lost in the quandary of decision trees and pathways that we will go mad and end up in a state of behavioral inertia. Our human brains do not have the capacity, attention, or working memory to explore all the possibilities. Dr. Damasio captures this paradox of choice through the experience of one of his patients who suffered damage to the area of his brain that processes emotion:

"I suggested two alternative dates, both in the coming month and just a few days apart from each other. The patient pulled out his appointment book and began consulting the calendar. The behavior that ensued, which was witnessed by several investigators, was remarkable. For the better part of a half an hour, the patient enumerated reasons for and against each of the two dates: previous engagements, proximity to other engagements, possible meteorological conditions, virtually anything that one could reasonably think about concerning a simple date… [He was] walking us through a tiresome cost benefit analysis, an endless outlining and fruitless comparison of options and possible consequences. It took enormous discipline to listen to all of this without pounding on the table and telling him to stop, but we finally did tell him, quietly, that he should come on the second of the alternative dates. His response was equally calm and prompt. He simply said: 'That's fine.' Back the appointment book went into his pocket, and he was off. This behavior is a good example of the limits of pure reason."

So, do we make good rational decisions? Unfortunately, we do not. We make decisions that we feel are good decisions. We make decisions in milliseconds or minutes, depending on the timeframe set as appropriate for the goal we want to achieve; to do that without pure reason we must have an alternative method, and that is our System 1 pathway.

Take the same abstract scenario as above, but this time before we apply any kind of cost/benefit analysis and before we start building decision trees with consequences and pathways, instead our emotional construct is providing feedback. When a potential bad consequence, real or perceived, comes to mind, we fleetingly and subconsciously experience an unpleasant emotion or feeling. When a potential good consequence surfaces, we experience a positive emotion or feeling, an incentive. This emotional feedback forces attention on the outcome and may quickly access a memory that further strengthens this emotional signal. The emotional feedback is an automated system providing degrees of positive and negative feelings. The emotional feedback may lead us to reject immediately a perceived negative option and choose from among the alternatives. The automated emotional feedback allows us to choose from among fewer options and surfaces options that have the best emotional positive outcome. There still is room for using a rational cost/benefit analysis, but only after the automated emotional feedback reduces the number of options.

What we know about System 1 feedback and its prevalence in impacting our decisions is that it affects the vast majority of our decisions. The choice presented to us as the one that produces the best possible emotional outcome is the choice we follow through with. We inherently and automatically acquiesce to the best emotional choice unless there is enough conflict to push the decision to the conscious mind and our System 2 pathway. We feel, behave, and lastly think out of neurobiological necessity. We are not able to solve for all of the possible outcomes, and we cannot solve for those consequences to arrive at a decision with any immediacy. Our System 1 process along with our emotional construct gives us an answer that we feel positive about so we can make the decision. By using a fast, associative, pattern-seeking system guided by emotion, we arrive at not necessarily the best decision, or the rational decision, but one that is okay most of the time. Because we can make quick decisions with incomplete information, we have gained an evolutionary advantage. Our decisions are better than a random choice, with enough accuracy to get us to behave with fewer negative consequences and pursue positive incentives.

When questioned by others or in preparation for justification to our peers, our conscious, rational self, our social human self, conveniently narrates a logical story as to why we behaved the way we did. We post-rationalize so that we can explain to others, to reaffirm a decision already made. Our social evolution has required that we explain a decision or behavior so that others can learn. We evolved through shared learning, and this is part of that mechanism. Ponder that for a moment; if we did not have to explain our decisions or behaviors, would we need to post-rationalize? It is difficult to recall a decision that I have made recently for which I have not created a reinforcing internal monologue. We are feeling and sensing organisms. Our brains rationalize what they have already felt and sensed.

Emotional Beings That Think

Our survival coincides with the greatest possible reduction of unpleasant body states and attaining functionally balanced biological states in what is called homeostatic balance: the ultimate Goldilocks game of keeping our bodies just right. Our internal preference system is inherently biased to avoid pain and seek pleasure, and to achieve these goals in a social environment. While there is an external set of circumstances which influence us—such as the conditions of our environment, the events relative to which we must act, possible options for actions, possible future outcomes of those actions, positive consequences or incentives, and negative consequences or deterrents—we are ultimately making decisions in pursuit of positive emotional outcomes.

Our emotions act as a biasing agent, always influencing how we behave. Like all biases, they can be wrong, and they can be extreme. On one end of the spectrum is being so overwhelmed with emotion that we cannot behave; for example, a fear of flying. The other end of the spectrum we explored through Dr. Damasio's patients and autism: being devoid of emotion, resulting in the inability to behave. Both examples demonstrate the role emotion plays in influencing our decision making. Our emotional response biases our cognitive process in a subconscious manner, which in turn influences any conscious reasoning or decision making.

Emotions automatically tell us what is important or unimportant based upon the degree of the consequence of the decision. Without the influence of emotion, we would be overwhelmed with the simplest of decisions, caught in an endless sequence of "what if" statements, like some rogue computer code that never stops generating possibilities. We in most situations do not have the capacity or time to rationally think, and we default to our fail safe: how we feel. Our emotional construct serves up a priority list of decisions, all with degrees of positive emotional outcomes. How can you go wrong about a decision that makes you feel good? Are you going to choose something that makes you feel bad? No, and that is why such choices can be eliminated so quickly as options. Our System 1 pathway is so efficient at narrowing the decision points to those that fit positive emotional patterns that it serves them up subconsciously. Whether it is a long-term brand affinity pattern, like the one demonstrated by my relationship with Crest toothpaste, or a short-term emotional pattern, as in the case of my ski boot purchase, the emotional motivation, consequences, and affirmations are behind the behavior. We are, after all, emotional beings that have the capability to think.

The Path Less Traveled

Emotion is what makes us human, and it impacts every conscious and subconscious decision we make. Timothy Wilson, professor of psychology at the University of Virginia and author of the book *Stranger to Ourselves*, says that we take in about 11 million bits of information every second, but we are consciously aware of about only 40 bits of that information. The remainder are being processed without us even knowing.

Our System 1 pathway and emotional construct constantly refines and reduces information so that we can be guided to the most efficient and positive emotional outcome. Our emotions impact our attention and memory, both of which guide what the conscious mind has available to process, should our System 2 pathway be called upon for assistance. Even our subconscious goals and motivations prompting our behavior are emotional in origin and part of our emotional construct's constant homeostatic feedback loop. We are dependent on emotional goals and motivations to behave even if the chosen behaviors are not in our rational best interest.

Without emotions we are unable to make decisions, left bewildered by endless "what if" scenarios and without understanding of the consequences. Tasks as simple as choosing what to eat for lunch or on which day to schedule an appointment are arduous decisions that slip from our grasp as incomprehensible. We feel what we see, as the world around us is automatically processed as visual information. We feel without any conscious knowledge that we are continuously processing emotion. We are so in tune with and reliant on emotion that not only can we feel what others feel, but we engage in emotional mimicry as a social adaptation function.

With all of this emotional feedback we assemble shortcuts: both cognitive biases and heuristics. These biases and heuristics provide quick System 1 paths from emotion to behavior. Our implicit feelings or beliefs guide how we behave and what we think. Implicit truths are our truths even if they stray from rational reality. To make sense of it all, we have the unique ability to create our own rational narrative to satiate the rational, conscious mind. Post-rationalization is our way of making sense of what was subconscious, and we employ it to convey to others why we behaved the way we did. We preemptively prepare a mental script to confirm our conformity to social, rational behavior should we be questioned why we behaved as we did.

I hope I have conveyed the overwhelming role that emotion plays in decision making and behavior and shown how consumer behavior can be impacted not by touting rational features and benefits but by appealing to the emotions that guide us to decision.

At the outset of this book, I put forth that the pathway to human decision making is that we feel, then behave, and lastly think. Our emotional construct is part of our System 1 pathway, operating in a fast, associative, involuntary, and subconscious manner. However, brands, marketers, and researchers do not account for the full pathway, focusing only on how consumers think or behave. They thus ignore the emotional origin of our behavior and focus on the post-rationalized narratives we all construct to explain why we behaved the way we did. This flaw I likened to looking into a room through a keyhole rather than opening the door. The view will always be incomplete no matter how you peer into the hole, distorted by the shape of the hole, the lighting, the shadows, and your own eyesight. You will see only what you are allowed to see. Unfortunately, this myopic view of the consumer is prevailing. How can we understand consumers when we ignore the human decision-making process? By understanding the feel, behave, think pathway, brands, marketing, and researchers can gain a holistic view of the decision process. If we have a more complete view of how people arrive at a decision, then we can influence and measure it with increased accuracy. We can improve our communications when we understand how the decision will be made.

My challenge to you is to open the door by utilizing the analytical framework of feel, behave, think. When we utilize all three lenses, we have a more holistic understanding of the consumer. We not only have more opportunity for insight, but we also begin to close the disconnect between what people say and what they do. To apply the framework is simply to consider all three pieces individually and the pathway as a whole.

- Are you considering, measuring, or capturing the entire pathway?
- Do you have a method for capturing and addressing emotional System 1 information?
- Do you have a method for capturing and addressing attitudinal System 2 information?

- Are you evaluating stated or observed behavior, long-term or short-term behavior?

We need to put the issue into the context and timeframe of the intended consumer behavior. Is the issue a brand question, something involving long-term affinity, where brand heuristics and implicit associations are key to the decision? Or is the issue something that is more short-term, such as a product packaging decision? Changing brand equity is not a quick process in a consumer's mind, but consideration and purchase of a new service or package design is a behavior we can impact and witness any change to rapidly. Each requires its own approach and implementation. The same consideration would come into play when evaluating messaging and communications. Is the intent to motivate behavior in the long or short term? What are the attitudes we want consumers to narrate back to us, and which emotions do we believe are connected to rational features and functions? I find it a good exercise to create a motivational pathway and use that as my starting point for evaluation. While we do not want to back into our hypothesis, the use of such a pathway does get all the pieces in front of us to consider.

Collecting and evaluating consumer attitudinal information may seem tried and true. We collect enough information to represent a particular group of consumers, apply some statistical testing, and there we go: we know what consumers think. But why do they think that way? How do we change the way they think? That is what needs to be addressed: the why. How consumers feel provides the impetus for what they think. Emotions are the why. Nothing shuts down a quantitative data discussion more quickly than the why question, typically from marketing or the creative agency. We do not know because we did not capture why.

We need to determine which System 1 tool is most appropriate. Implicit testing does not reveal the emotion, but it does reveal the cognitive biases and heuristics that are a result of the emotions. As explained previously, understanding implicit strengths and weaknesses allows us to identify potential barriers to behavior that would not be revealed directly with traditional attitudinal information. A barrier is a result of negative emotional feedback. There is a misalignment between the motivation, the goal, and the emotions evoked. From a behavioral economics point of view, can you remove the barrier? If not, can you address it through marketing and diminish the perceived barrier or counteract it with an implicit strength? I know it sounds a bit silly to say play to your strengths, but you would be surprised by how many brands are unaware of their strengths, let alone the barriers that prevent consumers from choosing their brand.

Visual semiotics reveals the emotions of the consumer and can be used strategically at the brand level and tactically at the product or service level. Visual semiotics explicates our brain's direct pathway from the visual cortex to the amygdala, as well as our brain's transference of all information into image representations. Visual semiotics reveals not only the set of emotions evoked by a particular stimulus, but also the strength of those emotions and the priority order in which we feel them. We do not feel emotions singly; instead, we experience degrees of emotions that interact with one another in a bundle.

We could also employ a motivational pathway laddering technique, projective questioning, facial coding, text-based sentiment analysis, and a host of clinical-setting neuro-measurement tools, including the fMRI.

Whatever tool is used, what is crucial is the intent to capture emotion and the acknowledgement of emotion's power. If you are not considering emotion or do not believe emotion is a factor, you are trapped behind the door, forever peering through the keyhole you have created. Any understanding or explanation of consumer behavior achieved without addressing emotion is fundamentally flawed. If we leave out the emotional why, we are just hypothesizing about the behavioral results through the self-created narratives of consumer attitudes.

Measuring, explaining, and understanding emotions is difficult. It is different than what has been done in the past. Some will say, we have made it this far—why change now? Unfortunately, the inertia is very real.

I leave you with a passage from John F. Kennedy's speech at Rice Stadium in Houston, Texas, on September 12, 1962. This speech was given during a time of change and struggle with the past, looking into an unknown future in the hands of a new generation that called for change to the status quo.

"We choose to go to the moon in this decade and do the other things, not because they are easy, but because they are hard, because that goal will serve to organize and measure the best of our energies and skills, because that challenge is one that we are willing to accept, one we are unwilling to postpone, and one which we intend to win, and the others, too.

Acknowledgements

Almost a year ago Ged Parton, CEO of Maru asked me to write a book that encapsulated our company philosophy and bring it to life. Full of ignorant bliss about the book writing process, I set off on this adventure. I would like to thank you for encouraging me to pursue writing this book and providing me with the time to research and write it. You had confidence in what I could do even when I had moments of self-doubt. I am forever grateful for this opportunity.

Abigail Aufgang for always being the positive voice of encouragement and willing to listen even when what I was saying made no sense. You kept me on pace with every milestone. In addition, you took on a much larger role in the company, filling the vacuum of my weekly hiatus. Your future success is unstoppable.

For the entire Maru organization who patiently provided me with room to write on Thursday's and Friday's, especially the North American executive team, in alphabetical order: Andrew Hawn; Brent Snider; Brian James; Dina Plahouras; Erica Ruyle; Jonathan Stinnett; Julie Paul; Kyle Davies; Liz Boyle; Michelle Walkey; Rich Durante; Sara Cappe; Ted Chen; Tommy Stinson.

Andrew Grenville who let me carve my own book writing path while providing a comfortable understanding of the process. The journal articles and additional books you provided, gave me material on those dark days when I needed that exact next piece.

Grant Heckman who patiently worked with me to transform the raw manuscript into a final product. Your attention to detail and suggestions have enriched this book. Any lack of clarity or mistakes someone may see in this book are mine alone.

Craig MacPherson and Megan Paul who guided me through the production and marketing. I never knew there was so much more to do.

To my wife Laura, who challenged me to write this book in a different way. For listening to the same stories for 30 years and still laughing. I would be lost without you. My boys: Hunter, Drew, and Spencer who had to listen to me work through sections of the book aloud and would often be unwittingly drawn into a prolonged discussion, when they just wanted to know when dinner was.

My brother Tyson, who always seemed to call me when I had hit a wall, looking for that next piece of research or inspiration. He always provided good ideas and would lighten the mood, laughing at what stories I had written. The combination of brotherly banter and Maine humor would always put me back on track.

Lastly, to my Mom and Dad who provided fodder for some of these stories as part of my life experience. I would not be who I am today without you.

References

Chapter One

Davis, M. (1997). Neurobiology of fear responses: The role of the amygdala. *The Journal of Neuropsychiatry and Clinical Neurosciences, 9, 382-402.*

Ekman, P. (2021). Universal emotions. https://www.paulekman.com/universal-emotions

Kahneman, D. (2011). *Thinking, fast and slow.* Farrar, Straus and Giroux.

Vogel, D.R., Dickson, G.W., & Lehman, J.A. (1986). Persuasion and the role of visual presentation support: The UM/3M study. http://thinktwicelegal.com/olio/articles/persuasion_article.pdf

Chapter Two

Brosch, T., Scherer, K.R., Grandjean, D., & Sander, D. (2013). The impact of emotion on perception, attention, memory, and decision-making. *Swiss Medical Weekly, 143.* doi: 10.4414/smw.2013.13786. PMID: 23740562

Chiew, K.S., & Braver, T.S. (2011). Positive affect versus reward: Emotional and motivational influences on cognitive control. *Frontiers in Psychology, 2, 279.* doi: 10.3389/fpsyg.2011.00279

Damasio, A. R. (1994). Descartes' error: *Emotion, reason, and the human brain.* G.P. Putnam.

Feinstein, J.S., Duff, M.C., & Tranel, D. (2010). Sustained experience of emotion after loss of memory in patients with amnesia. *Proceedings of the National Academy of Science, 107*(17),7674-7679.

Gladwell, M. (2005). *Blink : The power of thinking without thinking.* Little, Brown and Co.

Hirst, W., Phelps, E. A., Buckner, R. L., Budson, A. E., Cuc, A., Gabrieli, J. D. E., Johnson, M. K., Lustig, C., Lyle, K. B., Mather, M., Meksin, R., Mitchell, K. J., Ochsner, K. N., Schacter, D. L., Simons, J. S., & Vaidya, C. J. (2009). Long-term memory for the terrorist attack of September 11: Flashbulb memories, event memories, and the factors that influence their retention. *Journal of Experimental Psychology: General, 138*(2), 161–176. https://doi.org/10.1037/a0015527

LeDoux, J.E. (2007). Emotional memory. *Scholarpedia.* http://www.scholarpedia.org/article/Emotional_memory.

Squire, L.R. (2009). The legacy of patient H.M. for neuroscience. *Neuron, 61*(1), 6-9. doi: 10.1016/j.neuron.2008.12.023. PMID: 19146808; PMCID: PMC2649674

Tyng, C. M., Amin, H.U., Saad, M.N.M., & Malik, A.S. (2017). The influences of emotion on learning and memory. *Frontiers in Psychology, 8, 1454*. doi:10.3389/fpsyg.2017.01454

Chapter Three

Banker, S., Dunfield, D., Huang, A., & Prelac, D. (2021). Neural mechanisms of credit card spending. *Scientific Reports, 11.* https://doi.org/10.1038/s41598-021-83488-3

Custers, R., & Aarts, H. (2010). The unconscious will: How the pursuit of goals operates outside of conscious awareness. *Science, 329*(5987), 47-50. doi: 10.1126/science.1188595

Garbinsky, E.N., Gladstone, J.J., Nikolova, H., & Olson, J.G. (2020). Love, lies, and money: Financial infidelity in romantic relationships.

Journal of Consumer Research, 47(1), 1–24.
https://doi.org/10.1093/jcr/ucz052

Sanfey, A. G., Rilling, J. K., Aronson, J. A., Nystrom, L. E., & Cohen, J. D. (2003). The neural basis of economic decision-making in the Ultimatum Game. *Science, 300*(5626), 1755–1758.
https://doi.org/10.1126/science.1082976

Chapter Four

Diano, M., Celeghin, A., Bagnis, A., & Tamietto, M. (2017). Amygdala response to emotional stimuli without awareness: Facts and interpretations. *Frontiers in Psychology, 7*, 2029.
doi:10.3389/fpsyg.2016.02029

Dimberg, U., Thunberg, M., & Grunedal, S. (2002). Facial reactions to emotional stimuli: Automatically controlled emotional responses. *Cognition and Emotion, 16*(4), 449–472.
https://doi.org/10.1080/02699930143000356

Foroni, F., & Semin, G.R. (2011). When does mimicry affect evaluative judgment? *Emotion, 11*(3), 687-690. doi:10.1037/a0023163

Northoff, G., Heinzel, A., De Greck, M., Bermpohl, F., Dobrowolny, H., & Panksepp, J. (2006). Self-referential processing in our brain—A meta-analysis of imaging studies on the self. *Neuroimage, 31*, 440–457.
10.1016/j.neuroimage.2005.12.002

Pourtois, G., Schettino, A., & Vuilleumier, P. (2013). Brain mechanisms for emotional influences on perception and attention: What is magic and what is not. *Biological Psychology, 92*, 492–512. doi:
10.1016/j.biopsycho.2012.02.007

Steiner, J. E. (1973). The gustofacial response: Observation on normal and anencephalic newborn infants. In J. F. Bosma (Ed.), *Oral sensation and perception: Development in the fetus and infant: Fourth symposium.* U.S. Government Printing Office.

Tyng, C.M., Amin, H.U., Saad, M.N.M., & Malik, A.S. (2017). The influences of emotion on learning and memory. *Frontiers in Psychology, 8*, 1454. doi:10.3389/fpsyg.2017.01454

Vuilleumier, P. (2005). How brains beware: Neural mechanisms of emotional attention. *Trends in Cognitive Science, 9*(12), 585-94. doi: 10.1016/j.tics.2005.10.011. Epub 2005 Nov 10. PMID: 16289871

Winkielman, P., & Berridge, K.C. (2004). Unconscious emotion. *Current Directions in Psychological Science, 13*(3),120–123. doi:10.1111/j.0963-7214.2004.00288.x

Chapter Five

Wansink, B., & Sobal, J. (2007). Mindless eating: The 200 daily food decisions we overlook. *Environment and Behavior, 39*(1), 106–123. https://doi.org/10.1177/0013916506295573

Chapter Six

McClure, S.M., Li, J., Tomlin, D., Cypert, K.S., Montague, L.M., & Montague, P.R. (2004). Neural correlates of behavioral preference for culturally familiar drinks. *Neuron, 44*(2), 379-387. https://www.sciencedirect.com/science/article/pii/S0896627304006129

Chapter Seven

Bargh, J.A., Gollwitzer, P.M., Lee-Chai, A., Barndollar, K., & Trötschel, R. (2001). The automated will: Nonconscious activation and pursuit of behavioral goals. *Journal of Personality and Social Psychology, 81*(6), 1014–27. doi:10.1037/0022-3514.81.6.1014. PMC 3005626. PMID 11761304

Ben-Haim, M.S., Chajut, E., Hassin, R.R., & Algom, D. (2015). Speeded naming or naming speed? The automatic effect of object speed on performance. *Journal of Experimental Psychology: General, 144*(2), 326–38. doi:10.1037/a0038569. PMID 25559652

Brizendine, L. (2010). *The male brain: A breakthrough understanding of how men and boys think.* Random House.

Forbes, D. (2015). *The science of why: Decoding human motivation and transforming marketing strategy.* Palgrave Macmillan. doi:10.1057/9781137502049

Gallese, V., Fadiga, L., Fogassi, L., & Rizzolatti, G. (1996). Action recognition in the premotor cortex. *Brain, 119*(2), 593–609. https://doi.org/10.1093/brain/119.2.593

Gutman, J. (1997). Means-end chains as goal hierarchies. *Psychology and Marketing, 14*, 545-60.

Lanouette, W., & Silard, B.A. (1992). *Genius in the shadows: A biography of Leo Szilard, the man behind the bomb.* Charles Scribner's Sons.

Unit sales of the leading toothpaste vendors in the United States in 2020. (2021). Statista. https://www.statista.com/statistics/433656/leading-us-toothpaste-vendors/

Winerman, L. (2005). The mind's mirror. *American Psychological Association, 36*(9), 48. https://www.apa.org/monitor/oct05/mirror

Chapter Eight

Cheskin, L. (1951). *Color for profit.* Liveright.

Father daughter. (2010). https://www.youtube.com/watch?v=6F3-InOdMP4

For all your love. (2019). https://www.youtube.com/watch?v=57ByHtFrtlo

Gladwell, M. (2005). *Blink: The power of thinking without thinking*. Little, Brown and Co.

Making memories. (2017). https://www.youtube.com/watch?v=lmEkuACGSvk

Plassmann, H., O'Doherty, J., Shiv, B., & Rangel, A. (2008). Marketing actions can modulate neural representations of experienced pleasantness. *Proceedings of the National Academy of Sciences, 105*(3), 1050-1054. DOI: 10.1073/pnas.0706929105

Twilley, N. (November 2, 2015). Accounting for taste – How packaging can make food more flavorful. *New Yorker Magazine*.

Chapter Nine

Damasio, A. R. (1994). *Descartes' error: Emotion, reason, and the human brain*. G.P. Putnam.

Wilson, T. D. (2002). *Strangers to ourselves: Discovering the adaptive unconscious*. Belknap Press.